POWER
to
HEAL

8 KEYS TO ACTIVATING
God's Healing Power in Your Life

STUDY GUIDE

RANDY CLARK

DESTINY IMAGE® PUBLISHERS, INC.

P.O. Box 310, Shippensburg, PA 17257-0310

"Promoting Inspired Lives."

This book and all other Destiny Image and Destiny Image Fiction books are available at Christian bookstores and distributors worldwide.

For more information on foreign distributors, call 717-532-3040.

Reach us on the Internet: www.destinyimage.com.

ISBN 13 TP: 978-0-7684-0734-1

For Worldwide Distribution, Printed in the U.S.A.

2 3 4 5 6 7 8 / 19 18 17 16 15

SESSIONS

HOW TO USE YOUR STUDY GUIDE

The *Power to Heal* study guide is divided into eight sessions and includes 40 days of reinforcement devotionals.

Each week, study participants will:

1) Watch a Group Session. These weekly sessions are designed to be watched in a group or class setting, or by a single individual, however, a group setting is highly recommended as it will enable you to maximize the material presented. These sessions will consist of:

   a. Summary of the weekly session.

   b. Discussion Questions for group/class/individual discussion and reflection.

   c. Group Activation Exercise: After watching the session, taking notes, and engaging in discussion, you will take what you have learned and put it to work in the context of your small group or class.

2) Keep up with daily exercises. These daily activities are designed to reinforce the material you learned during the Group Sessions. They consist of the following:

   a. Devotional reading: Daily devotional segments offer an outlet for increased clarification of the week's topics, and provide opportunity for meditation.

   b. Reflection questions: These are designed to help you critically interact with the material you are learning in the sessions.

   c. Prayer directive: Healing ministry starts in the place of prayer. These short, simple prayer topics help you give voice to the empowering work of the Holy Spirit in your life.

SESSION 1

ACTIVATE

RECEIVE AND RELEASE GOD'S HEALING POWER

The power of the Holy Spirit is available.
It's within you.
You simply need to step out, believe you are anointed, trust
that God wants to use you, and start taking risks.

~

But you shall receive power when the Holy Spirit
has come upon you.
—ACTS 1:8

SESSION 1 SUMMARY

You are already filled with the Holy Spirit. When you received Jesus as your Lord and Savior, the person of the Holy Spirit came to dwell inside of you. To activate God's healing power, you simply need to believe in what you have already received and ask the Lord to release His power through you. This usually comes in an experience called the baptism of the Holy Spirit. Sadly, many believers never activate God's healing power in their lives because they have either been given incorrect information about healing or they have simply not been told about it at all.

In this session, you will receive a solid biblical foundation for healing the sick. Divine healing is not a side issue for the Christian to either accept or reject; it is a key part of fully preaching the gospel of Jesus Christ. This is revealed in both the ministry of Jesus and the vibrant demonstration of the early church. God has not changed His program.

DISCUSSION QUESTIONS

1. Read Matthew 11:12. What does it look like to forcefully or violently lay hold of God's Kingdom?

2. What do you think it looks like for God to "show Himself strong" through you (see 2 Chron. 16:9)?

3. What do you currently believe about God's healing power?

   a. He healed in the past during biblical times, but He does not heal anymore.

   b. He still heals, but we should not expect it to be normal.

4. Why do you think so many Christians have a difficult time embracing their role in healing ministry?

5. In Hebrews 6:1–2, we read about multiple baptisms. How do you understand the difference between these baptisms?

6. What is your definition and understanding of the baptism of the Holy Spirit?

7. Read Luke 24:49. As you prepare to step out in healing ministry, why do you think receiving a fresh baptism of the Holy Spirit's power is so important?

8. Share. Have willing group/class members share their testimonies of being baptized in the Holy Spirit. Specifically ask for those who have experienced multiple baptisms in the Spirit (like Randy did), and how those encounters impacted their lives.

GROUP ACTIVATION EXERCISE

Do not get drunk on wine, which leads to debauchery. Instead, be filled with the Spirit (Ephesians 5:18 NIV).

Today, you are going to cry out for a fresh baptism of the Holy Spirit to come upon your life. It does not matter if you have been filled with the Holy Spirit for decades, or if this is your first time being introduced to the experience. In order to release God's power, you need to be filled to overflowing with His presence over and over again.

Even though the disciples were born again and saved because of their faith in Jesus, He still told them to wait in Jerusalem to receive power from on high. Later on in the book of Acts, we see the early disciples being filled at Pentecost and refilled in Acts 4. *There is always more* of the Holy Spirit to be experienced. Every encounter should bring us into a deeper level of fruitfulness.

Remember that the baptism of the Spirit is not for a feeling. It is also more than just receiving one specific gift of the Spirit. Press in for a fresh baptism of the Spirit today, being hungry and expectant for a fresh demonstration of God's healing power through your life.

WEEKLY READING ASSIGNMENT

Be sure to read Chapters 1–4 in *Power to Heal* this week and complete your study guide assignments.

SESSION NOTES

_____

_____

_____

_____

_____

_____

_____

_____

_____

_____

_____

_____

_____

_____

_____

_____

_____

_____

JESUS IS OUR MODEL FOR LIFE AND MINISTRY

Most assuredly, I say to you, he who believes in Me,
the works that I do he will do also....
JOHN 14:12

If you believe in Jesus, then you are called and empowered to do the same works that He did while He was physically present upon the earth. This commission comes directly from the words of Jesus. It is not locked into a certain period of history or dispensation; it is the normative expectation of all believers throughout all of time to do the works of Jesus, which includes healing the sick.

What keeps many of us from participating in the healing ministry is the fact that we have looked to other models instead of looking to Jesus. Perhaps, a church, ministry, denomination, or theological thought process has influenced our idea of what it means to fully preach the gospel. For many people, healing or deliverance is not even part of this equation.

You've heard it said, "Perhaps God still heals. Maybe there are a few people living in remote parts of the world suffering demonic torment. But certainly, such things should *not* be considered normative experiences in the Christian life." Does this sound like something that Jesus would say or preach?

Set the standard of Christian ministry by fixing your eyes on the Author and Finisher of your faith—Jesus (see Heb. 12:1–2). He alone is what we measure our lives and ministries by. What Jesus did, we have been invited to do as well.

REFLECTION QUESTIONS

1. If Jesus is your model for the Christian life and ministry, how does this change the way you view healing?

_____

_____

_____

_____

_____

_____

2. Are there any barriers in your theology or thought process that keep you from embracing your commission to release God's healing power? If so, what are they? Write these ideas down and measure them beside the standard of Jesus. (Remember, Jesus Christ is our perfect model for life and ministry. If our theology does not agree with who Jesus is or what Jesus did, we need to adapt our theology to His standard.)

_____

_____

_____

_____

_____

_____

PRAYER DIRECTIVE

Ask the Lord to give you a fresh glimpse of Jesus and His example of healing ministry.

DIVINE HEALING WAS PROVIDED IN THE ATONEMENT

Surely He took up our pain and bore our suffering, yet we considered Him punished by God, stricken by Him, and afflicted. But He was pierced for our transgressions, He was crushed for our iniquities; the punishment that brought us peace was on Him, and by His wounds we are healed (Isaiah 53:4–5 NIV).

In our fallen world, all kinds of illnesses, injuries, and emotional dysfunctions abound. Medical help benefits many, although sometimes improvement from medical help is slow, and, in some cases, it is even ineffective. For others, medical help is not available or it is not even desired. For these and many other reasons, countless people have an interest in seeking divine healing. What provision has God made for effective healing through prayer? The answer is that healing, like salvation, has been provided for in the atonement.

It is familiar theology that Jesus, by giving His life on the cross, paid the price for our salvation—that Jesus took on Himself the penalty for our sins, and that through faith in Him we can be saved from punishment for our sins and moved from eternal death to eternal life. It is perhaps less familiar theology that Jesus, in His atoning work on the cross, also paid the price for the healing of physical and emotional illnesses. Isaiah 53 confirms this.

REFLECTION QUESTIONS

1. Read Matthew 8:16–17. How did Jesus specifically fulfill the prophecy written in Isaiah 53?

_____

_____

_____

_____

_____

_____

_____

2. As you understand that the cross made provision for sickness as well as for sin, how does this change the way you will pray for the sick in the days to come?

_____

_____

_____

_____

_____

_____

_____

_____

_____

_____

_____

_____

PRAYER DIRECTIVE

Father, open my eyes to the finished work of Jesus on the cross. Help me to get a full vision of everything He suffered and died for.

JESUS'S MISSION IS YOUR MISSION

≈≈

...how God anointed Jesus of Nazareth with the Holy Spirit and
with power, who went about doing good and healing all who
were oppressed by the devil, for God was with Him.
—ACTS 10:38

Consider this passage of Scripture for just a moment. Jesus healed the sick because He desired to bring freedom to all who were oppressed by the devil. After Jesus rose from the dead, and just before He ascended back into heaven, He told the disciples, *"As the Father has sent Me, I also send you"* (John 20:21). After giving them this commission, we read that He breathed upon them and they received the Holy Spirit.

This is also our commission. Each one of us are being sent to bring healing to those who are being oppressed by the devil in our sphere of influence. In order to do this, we need to be confident in the power of God at work inside of us. You have received the same Holy Spirit who anointed and empowered Jesus. With this in mind, I encourage you to step out, assured that the power of God in you will back you up. You don't have the ability to heal anyone—right up front, you must come to terms with this. Rather, it is the One inside of you who does the work of healing. Trust Him and remember that the Spirit who enabled Jesus to heal is also inside of you.

REFLECTION QUESTIONS

1. When you read Acts 10:38, what are your thoughts? Do you have a difficult time with the idea that you can also do the same works as Jesus? If so, I encourage you to spend some time with the Lord and ask Him to change the way you think about this matter.

_____

_____

_____

_____

_____

_____

_____

_____

2. Read Romans 8:11. If the same Spirit who raised Jesus from the dead lives inside of you, how does this impact the way you approach healing?

_____

_____

_____

_____

_____

_____

_____

_____

_____

PRAYER DIRECTIVE

Holy Spirit, just as You anointed Jesus to do the supernatural works of ministry, You live inside of me, empowering me to do the same works. Jesus healed the sick because of Your power at work in Him. You live in me, which means I can also release Your healing power to those in need as well!

UNLEASH THE LIVING WATER

Water is often a symbol for the Holy Spirit throughout Scripture. In the Gospel of John, we read about two kinds of living water: There is a living water that is within, and then later we read of a living water that is released. These are both pictures of the presence of the Holy Spirit within you. One is a type of baptism into Christ, when we are born again and receive the Holy Spirit; the other is a picture of our baptism *in* the Holy Spirit, where we become vessels of His power on the earth.

REFLECTION AND MEDITATION

Today, I want you to spend some time in quiet reflection before the Lord. Read and meditate on John 4:10–12 and John 7:37–39.

Living Water Within:

> *Jesus answered and said to her, "If you knew the gift of God, and who it is who says to you, 'Give Me a drink,' you would have asked Him, and He would have given you living water." The woman said to Him, "Sir, You have nothing to draw with, and the well is deep. Where then do You get that living water? Are You greater than our father Jacob, who gave us the well, and drank from it himself, as well as his sons and his livestock?"* (John 4:10–12)

1. What do you think this living water is a picture of?

_____

_____

_____

_____

_____

_____

_____

_____

_____

Living Water Released:

> *On the last day, that great day of the feast, Jesus stood and cried out, saying, "If anyone thirsts, let him come to Me and drink. He who believes in Me, as the Scripture has said, out of his heart will flow rivers of living water." But this He spoke concerning the Spirit, whom those believing in Him would receive; for the Holy Spirit was not yet given, because Jesus was not yet glorified (John 7:37–39).*

2. What do you think this living water is a picture of? Why do you think the language of *rivers* and *flowing* are significant in this expression of living water?

_____

_____

_____

_____

_____

_____

_____

_____

PRAYER DIRECTIVE

Ask the Holy Spirit to give you a picture of what it means to be filled with His presence. Sometimes, we as believers take this great privilege for granted. The truth is that God has made a home inside of each one of us. We have received living water—the Holy Spirit—so that we can *release* the rivers of living water to those around us.

GET FILLED AND REFILLED

And do not be drunk with wine, in which is dissipation; but be filled with the Spirit.
—EPHESIANS 5:18)

Paul sets an example here on how we should constantly be pressing in for more of God. It should be a continuous lifestyle of crying out for an increased filling with the Holy Spirit. Paul's language here is basically saying, "Be constantly filled with the Spirit." This is definitely not a one-time deal. God does not want you and me to simply arrive at one place and coast for the rest of our lives. Sadly, this is all too common for many believers today.

For some, the quest stops at salvation. They get saved, and through the teaching they are exposed to or the ideas they entertain, they are convinced that going to heaven is the pinnacle of the Christian life—that there is really nothing for them to do on earth. As a result, they either fall into bondage of strict legalism, reducing following Jesus to adhering to a moral code, or they are convinced they can live any way they want, since their eternity has already been settled. There is really no motivation for them to press into anything *more* while living on earth.

We press in for more when we first have a vision for it. Salvation is the beginning of the Christian life, not the end of it. For others, perhaps they pressed into more of God, but once they received the baptism of the Holy Spirit, or spoke in tongues, or prophesied one time, they got the idea that there is nowhere else to go. I want to encourage you to trust that, wherever you are today, God has more for you. *There is more!*

REFLECTION QUESTIONS

1. What does it mean to be *continually filled* with the Holy Spirit? What do you think this looks like in your daily life?

_____

_____

_____

_____

_____

2. Read Acts 4:23–31. How is this an example of the disciples being *filled again* with the Holy Spirit? What specifically did the disciples ask to accompany their bold proclamation of the gospel?

_____

_____

_____

_____

_____

_____

_____

PRAYER DIRECTIVE

Use Acts 4:29–30 as a model prayer and ask the Lord for a fresh baptism of the Holy Spirit. Maybe this is the first time have prayed for this experience; maybe you have had *many* fillings with the Spirit. It does not matter—there is always more! You can pray something like:

Father, I ask for an increase of the presence and power of the Holy Spirit in my life. Fill me anew. Spirit of the Living God, fall fresh upon me. I am not content coasting through my Christian life, drawing from yesterday's experience.

Give me a vision for more. As I go through this study, open my eyes. Show me the great and wondrous things You want to do in the earth through Your people—through me!

More than anything else, Lord, I want to see You receive the glory You deserve. As I step out in Your power and see the sick get healed, this glorifies Your name. Signs, wonders, and miracles bring You great glory, Father. I desire to participate in this. But to do this, I need Your power. I can't heal the sick. I don't have the power in myself—but You do, and You live inside of me.

Baptize me, Holy Spirit. Use me to represent Jesus by bringing His Kingdom and compassion to the sick. In Jesus's name, amen.

SESSION 2

INTIMACY

Discover and Experience the Healing Ways of God

Healings and miracles are the byproducts of those who enjoy intimate fellowship with God and are committed to doing His works. To do His works, we first need to know His ways. Who are the ones who press in to know the ways of God? Those whose great prize in life is intimacy with the Father.

He made known His ways to Moses, His acts to the children of Israel.
—Psalm 103:7 ESV

SESSION 2 SUMMARY

When we intimately discover the ways of God, we learn how to accurately represent Him in the world and fully give the Father the glory He deserves. In this foundational session, you will learn that supernatural healing is not a side or peripheral issue for the Christian life. Not only is healing one of the key works that Jesus performed, but it is likewise a work He expects His followers to walk in too. Healing is also a visible demonstration of a life saturated in God's presence. More than pursuing miracles, supernatural experiences, or some kind of Holy Spirit thrill ride, we are to be like Moses, who cried out for God to show him His ways.

As you walk in God's healing power, remember that you are representing His character and nature. You are showing the world a visible expression of Jesus Christ—the hope of glory. You are bearing fruit that brings God great glory. Healing is not just about people being cured of their infirmities, afflictions, and diseases. That is surely one dimension. But the other side is that healings and miracles are one of the primary ways that God has received glory throughout Scripture.

DISCUSSION QUESTIONS

1. John 14–17 represents the last words of Jesus. Why is it important for us to pay careful attention to what He said in these chapters?

2. Read John 14:12–13. Why are "plain and simple" Bible verses like this challenging to us (specifically, in regards to healing and miracles)?

   a. Who is Jesus speaking to in John 14?

   b. Why is it so important for you to know that God has made His healing power available to everyone, not just the disciples who walked with Him while He was on the earth?

3. Read John 15:7. What does it mean to abide in God's words? How do His words release faith inside of you?

4. How does a freshly spoken word of God release faith in you to do what God is asking (inspiration versus revelation)?

5. How is it possible for you to do greater works today?

6. Why do you need both the fruit of the Spirit *and* the gifts of the Spirit (not one without the other)?

7. Read John 14:13. How does walking in signs, wonders, and supernatural works bring glory to God the Father?

8. What does it mean to *ask* in Jesus's name, and how does this relate to knowing God's character?

GROUP ACTIVATION EXERCISE

Most assuredly, I say to you, he who believes in Me, the works that I do he will do also; and greater works than these he will do, because I go to My Father (John 14:12).

Break up into groups of two and pray for each other to step into greater encounters with the ways of God. You can pray specifically for:

- Increased intimacy with God.

- Greater revelation of the ways of God.

- A hunger to walk in the greater works of Jesus.

- Fresh passion for God's Word, both the freshly spoken words (inspiration) and the Scriptures (revelation).

- Deeper understanding of God's character and nature, so you can pray in a way that honors His name.

If the Holy Spirit starts to speak prophetically through the person praying for you, write it down. Likewise, if you begin to receive a prophetic word for the person you are praying for, *share it with them.*

The goal of this session is to pursue greater levels of intimacy with God. It is in the place of intimacy where you hear His voice, learn His ways, and encounter His deep compassion.

WEEKLY READING ASSIGNMENT

Be sure to read Chapters 5–7 in *Power to Heal* this week and complete your study guide assignments.

SESSION NOTES

_____

_____

_____

_____

_____

_____

_____

_____

_____

_____

_____

_____

_____

Day Six

FRIENDS OF GOD

〰️

The friendship of the Lord is for those who fear Him,
and He makes known to them His covenant.
—Psalm 25:14 ESV

What was Moses's secret to knowing and experiencing the ways of God? Intimacy. While Israel witnessed the miraculous acts of God—which were outstanding and supernatural in and of themselves—Moses *knew* God personally. One of the very identities that God revealed to Moses was *"I am the Lord who heals you"* (Exod. 15:26). To move in healing power, we first need to intimately know the Healer. To see God's acts is one thing; to know His ways reveals a much deeper level of closeness. Anyone can watch a miracle happen, but it takes another kind of person to know *why* the miracle happened. This revelation is reserved for God's friends.

In Exodus 33:11, we see that *the Lord would speak to Moses face to face, as one speaks to a friend* (NIV). God reveals His ways to His friends. Under the Old Testament, these were few and far between. Moses and Abraham are the only two people who are described as friends of God under the Old Covenant. This is why Jesus's revelation to His disciples in John 15:14–15 is so incredible. A significant paradigm shift was taking place, where a divine communion was available only to a select, elite few was now being opened up to all. Jesus said,

You are My friends if you do whatever I command you. No longer do I call you servants, for a servant does not know what his master is doing; but I have called you friends, for all things that I heard from My Father I have made known to you.

DRAW NEAR

Instead of asking specific study questions, I want you to take this week to cultivate intimacy with God. A good starting place is taking a small portion of Scripture and asking the Holy Spirit to show you His ways in those particular verses.

SCRIPTURE FOR MEDITATION

Read Exodus 15:26. What does this passage reveal about God's nature as the Healer? More than seeing healings take place, or being used to release healing, why do you think it is important to intimately know God's character and nature as the Healer?

_____

_____

_____

_____

_____

_____

_____

_____

_____

_____

_____

_____

_____

_____

_____

_____

_____

HOW GOD RECEIVES GLORY

Most assuredly, I say to you, he who believes in Me, the works that I do he will do also; and greater works than these he will do, because I go to My Father. And whatever you ask in My name, that I will do, that the Father may be glorified in the Son.
—John 14:12–13

Jesus taught that one of the primary ways the Father receives glory is when the church does the works that Jesus did. If you read John 14–16 in its context, you will see that Jesus is not just talking about works that we can do in our natural ability. He is talking about works that demand supernatural enablement, or supernatural grace. These kinds of works can only be accomplished in the power of the Holy Spirit, and when they are done they bring glory to God.

In view of this insight, rest assured that it is not a flaky charismatic thing to desire to move in the power and gifts of the Holy Spirit. It is just as honorable and noble as walking in the fruit of the Spirit. Desiring to move in the gifts and power of the Spirit is essential to bringing glory to God. The motivation in our pursuit of letting God release His power through us is the glory of God.

Christians, by and large, want to bring glory to God. Regardless of what theological or denominational tradition you come from, there is a deep desire inside of you to please God. In one sense, God is pleased with you because you stand justified and righteous before Him through the blood of Jesus. However, we get to participate in God's pleasure. On earth we get to *give God glory* by performing the works He has commissioned us to do. It would seem that studying these passages of Scripture in context, these works include signs, wonders, miracles, and healings!

SCRIPTURE MEDITATION

Read John 14:13. How do you think healing miracles bring glory to the Father through His Son?

GREATER INTIMACY, GREATER WORKS

Most assuredly, I say to you, he who believes in Me, the works that I do he will do also; and greater works than these he will do, because I go to My Father.
—JOHN 14:12

The Scriptures that often give us the most difficulty are not the "hard to understand" passages; it's the black and white, crystal clear biblical directives that challenge reality as we know it. This verse in John 14:12 is an enormous invitation, given from the heart of God. Many of us would be content just seeing and participating in the *same* works of Jesus. Here, however, Jesus is actually inviting us into more. Is there some key to walking in these "greater works?" I don't think it has anything to do with a formula or principle. Rather, the greater works belong to those who walk in greater intimacy with God, not those who are performing *for* God in a greater work. It's those who are simply friends of the Holy Spirit.

Study the lives of the great healing evangelists: John G. Lake, Smith Wigglesworth, and Kathryn Kuhlman (to name just a few). Before they walked in healing power, they considered themselves close intimates with the Holy Spirit. He was their desire. They celebrated the miracles but pursued a person. God is looking for those who prize His presence above all else, for it is those He can entrust with the "greater works" because He knows the "greater" won't become a distraction.

It's true: there are some people who get distracted from Jesus because they are overly focused on supernatural phenomena, demonstrations, manifestations, etc. That does not mean we dismiss God's power. It only means we dive deeper into the place of fellowship and intimacy with Him, longing to know His ways and see His character expressed in the world.

SCRIPTURE MEDITATION

Read John 14:12. Backtrack a verse and focus today on Jesus's invitation to do greater works. How do you think intimacy with God plays a role in us walking in the "greater works" that Jesus describes here?

CHRIST IN YOU, THE HOPE OF GLORY

To them God has chosen to make known among the Gentiles the glorious riches of this mystery, which is Christ in you, the hope of glory.
—COLOSSIANS 1:27 NIV

Think about how close God came to you. He is not just *with* you—but because of the Holy Spirit, He actually dwells in you (see John 14:17). There is really no closer He can get than that. It is deception for us to think that God is *out there, somewhere*, almost as if He exists off in outer space. There is a dimension, a reality, a realm called heaven, and this is the place where God dwells. Paul the apostle was taken up into this place, where he encountered inexpressible wonders (see 2 Cor. 12:2). Heaven is an actual, real place. This is one side of reality. The other side is that God has given you a special gift from heaven to empower you to represent the Kingdom of heaven *on earth*. This gift is the person of the Holy Spirit, and He makes this reality—Christ in you—possible.

Scripture also tells us that Jesus is seated at the Father's right hand. So how can Christ actually be inside of you and seated at the Father's right hand? This takes place through the communion and fellowship of the Holy Spirit. The language of John 14–17 opens our eyes to the fellowship of the Trinity. Though it may be beyond full comprehension, this much we know: The Father is in the Son, the Son is in the Father, and both are in the Spirit. They exist in complete unity and communion. The Spirit who lives in union with the Father and Son has been sent to earth to dwell inside of you and make it possible for *you* to display the person of Jesus Christ.

SCRIPTURE MEDITATION

Read John 14:17. The disciples had the Holy Spirit *with them* at the time because Jesus was with them (and the Spirit was in Jesus). After Jesus accomplished the work of redemption, He made it possible for the Spirit to actually *live in* them…and in you. Today, spend some time thinking about how close God has come to you. How could this revelation of His closeness impact the way you pray for healing?

_____

_____

_____

_____

_____

_____

_____

_____

_____

_____

_____

_____

_____

_____

_____

_____

_____

_____

Day Ten

BEARING FRUIT, BRINGING GLORY

*By this My Father is glorified, that you bear much
fruit; so you will be My disciples.*
—JOHN 15:8

In Jesus's words, we see that the way in which we bring glory to the Father is by bearing much fruit. When we bear fruit, we reveal that we are truly Jesus's disciples. This is simple, but what does it say about church life when this is not happening? At a root level, the lack of fruit is the result of the lack of intimacy with God. If we are not pressing in to know the ways of God, we are not equipped to represent Him in the world through bearing fruit. As Jesus explained, "fruit" is the result of abiding, or remaining, in Him (see John 15:1–8).

What is the fruit that Jesus is speaking of? It is nothing other than works that represent the character of Jesus in the world. In Galatians 5, we read about the fruit of the Spirit. These are what I call the fruit of *being*. They are results of us *being Christians*. As we yield to the Spirit in our lives, He produces the character of Jesus in us. In John 15, however, we learn about a different kind of fruit. It is a fruit of *doing*. Do not misunderstand this, though. The fruit is still produced through *abiding* and *remaining in* Jesus. This time, however, intimacy produces demonstrative works. These include signs, wonders, miracles, and healings. Intimacy with God exposes us to His ways. When we know His ways, a desire is birthed within us to see these ways known in the earth (see Ps. 67:2). One way that God is known in the earth is through healing.

When the Christian life is reduced to upholding good morals and religious duty, this type of "life" does not bring the full amount of glory to the Father. Our quest and desire for spiritual gifts and supernatural power is not so that we can have "a good feeling." Rather, it is so that our lives will bring God the full measure of glory that He deserves.

SCRIPTURE MEDITATION

Read John 15:1–8. Describe how spending time with God—getting to know His character, His nature, and His ways—directly relates to you walking in His power and bearing fruit through seeing people healed?

SESSION 3

PRAY

USE THE FIVE-STEP PRAYER MODEL

There are many different ways of praying for the sick. The following five-step prayer model is not the only one. If you have found one that is effective for you, I encourage you to use it in your own personal ministry. If you are just starting out praying for healing, the five-step model is a simple, easy, and clear model for you to get going.

They will lay hands on the sick, and they will recover.
—MARK 16:18

SESSION 3 SUMMARY

The rest of the study guide is designed to help you sustain the healing ministry of Jesus in your life or church. Sustaining is great, but right now it's time to get you started ministering to the sick. By familiarizing yourself with the five-step prayer model, you are being equipped to step out with confidence. Perhaps this is the most important decision you can make that will lead to results in ministering to the sick. There are many believers who doctrinally believe in God's desire to heal the sick. Their theology is correct, but they are not putting it into practice. This is often because they don't have confidence in stepping out and actually praying for the sick.

As you learn about the five-step prayer model, you are being given a starting point. Do not turn this into a formula or law. You will quickly discover that God frequently operates outside of the parameters we set for Him with our manmade principles. This does not mean principles or templates like this are bad. We need to know the purpose they serve—a point of departure. This week, you are being launched into the healing ministry. With that commission comes a resource—this prayer model.

GROUP ACTIVATION EXERCISE

Today, you will discuss the five-step prayer model and practice on each other. Instead of going through discussion questions, you will focus on activation. The video session was designed to inform you for this very purpose. Now it is time to step out and put what you have learned into practice.

Practice taking each other through the five-step prayer model, as this will give you confidence in taking someone else through the model. This is not intended to merely be a role-playing experiment. It is designed to get you comfortable as you explain the process to someone else, and as you commit it to memory. The only way you will begin to internalize this prayer model, and ultimately start customizing it, is with practice.

1. Break up into groups of two (preferably, men with men and women with women).

2. You can either role-play or engage the process with an actual healing need. If one of you really needs healing prayer for a certain condition, if you feel comfortable, you can use this exercise as your chance to go through the model using a real-life situation.

3. Take about twenty-five to thirty minutes to go through this. (I would encourage group leaders or class teachers to print out copies of the five-step prayer model, which is included here in the study guide following these instructions.)

4. When you are finished going through the model, come back as a group/class and discuss your progress.

WEEKLY READING ASSIGNMENT

Be sure to read Chapters 8–9 in *Power to Heal* this week and complete your study guide assignments. Each of your daily devotional readings and exercises will focus on one step of the five-step prayer model. The goal is for you to become comfortable with the model, internalize the process, and ultimately customize it based on the different situations you find yourself ministering in. This week's activities will be more interactive than informational.

SESSION NOTES

THE FIVE-STEP PRAYER MODEL

BASIC OVERVIEW

1. Interview: Identify what kind of condition or sickness the person is dealing with, and evaluate what form of prayer is most appropriate for the situation.

2. Prayer selection: Based on what you learn in the interview, choose the kind of prayer you will use. Two of the most frequent prayers for healing are petition and command.

3. Prayer: Pray for the person's condition. The goal is to be as informed and specific as possible. Watch for what God is doing!

4. Reinterview and continue to pray for effect: Determine if there is any noticeable progress in the person you are praying for. If so, celebrate what God is doing. If not, go back through the process and try to evaluate what might be preventing the healing.

5. Post prayer suggestions: Encourage the people you pray for to effectively cooperate with God to see His healing power increased in their lives.

STEP ONE: THE INTERVIEW

Briefly interview the person who is requesting healing prayer. Be attentive and gentle. A loving attitude on your part will do much to reassure the person that he or she is in good hands. Remember, whether the people you pray for are healed or not, it is most important that because of their interactions with you they leave feeling loved.

1. Why should you ask people questions before you start praying for them?

    _____

    _____

    _____

    _____

    _____

2. Ask questions, such as:

    *   "What is your name?" (A question or two to put the person at ease.)

    *   "What would you like prayer for?"

    *   "How long have you had this condition?"

    *   "Do you know what the cause is?"

    *   "Have you seen a doctor?"

    *   "What does he or she say is the matter with you?"

    *   "Do you remember what was happening in your life when this condition started?"

    *   "Did anything traumatic happen to you about the time your condition began, or within a few months prior to it starting?"

ACTIVATE—INTERVIEW THE PERSON SO YOU CAN LEARN THE SPECIFICS

As you get ready to pray for healing, be sure to ask people questions so you can properly identify their condition. The more specific you can be, the better. The more clarity you have on the nature of their sickness, the more effectively you can minister to them. Knowing the specifics will help you:

- Be able to share a personal testimony or healing story in Scripture that would relate to the sickness or condition.

- Directly address by name whatever the sickness or condition is that is afflicting the person.

- Evaluate if the root of the condition is demonic in origin; and, if so, treat it as a spirit of affliction and cast it out.

If there are people in your life the Holy Spirit is directing you to pray for, approach them, and, before praying, ask questions that will help you evaluate their condition. Get comfortable with this process, for it will be very helpful in ministering to the sick.

STEP TWO: PRAYER SELECTION

In step two, the prayer selection, it is time to decide what type of prayer is most appropriate given the person and their needs. The two most common kinds of prayer to use when praying for the sick are the petition prayer and the command prayer. We must work with the Holy Spirit and specifically ask for His discernment as to which one to use.

Petition: A request to heal, addressed to God, to Jesus, or to the Holy Spirit.

- "Father, in the name of Jesus, I ask You to restore sight to this eye."

- "Father, I pray in Jesus's name, come and straighten this spine."

- "Father, release Your power to heal in Jim's body, in the name of Jesus."

- "Come, Holy Spirit. Release Your power. Touch Jim's back, in Jesus's name."

Command: A command addresses to a condition of the body, or a part of the body, or a troubling spirit, such as a spirit of pain, or infirmity, or affliction.

- "In the name of Jesus, I command this tumor to shrivel up and dissolve."

- "In the name of Jesus, spine, be straight! Be healed!"

- "In Jesus's name, I command every afflicting spirit: get out of Jim's body."

- "In the name of Jesus, I command all pain and swelling to leave this ankle."

ACTIVATE—CHOOSE THE KIND OF PRAYER THAT IS MOST APPROPRIATE

Learn how to build on the five-step prayer model every time you pray. You may not have the opportunity to pray for a sick person each day. This is why over the next few weeks, even as you go through the other sessions, it is important to keep coming back to the five-step prayer model.

After you interview someone, determine what the most effective kind of prayer would be for that specific situation. This is where you must consult the Holy Spirit for discernment and direction.

STEP THREE: PRAYER MINISTRY

The most important part of prayer ministry is that you move and operate *in the Spirit*. You can actually pray *in the Spirit* and not pray in tongues. Praying in tongues is one aspect of praying *in the Spirit*, but it is not the whole of it. Another essential expression of praying in the Spirit is praying under the active, influential leading of the Holy Spirit.

Once you conduct the interview and have decided on what kind of prayer to use, invite the Holy Spirit to come and give you supernatural wisdom in praying under His anointing. The *Power to Heal* book contains more practical detail on helping the person you are praying for receive healing most effectively. This is very important, but even more fundamental is your personal surrender to the Holy Spirit. It doesn't matter how you feel. It doesn't matter if the condition seems beyond your ability. The greatest thing you can do is to yield to the Holy Spirit, moment by moment, as you pray for the sick.

When you first step out in healing ministry, the Holy Spirit may take you "off script" but, chances are, He will keep you operating within the bounds of what you know until you have developed greater confidence to hear His voice. I am not advocating that this prayer model or any model be elevated above the leading of the Spirit. This model simply gives you a clear blueprint so you can step out with confidence. In that process of stepping out, however, simply recognize your constant state of dependence upon the Holy Spirit. He is all you offer the person you are praying for. The results are in God's hands. The best thing you can do is pray with an ear open to the Spirit's voice, following His direction, speaking out any words He places in your spirit, and moving in sync with His activity.

ACTIVATE—PRAY IN THE SPIRIT BEFORE YOU PRAY FOR HEALING

Learn to pray for people under the influence of the Holy Spirit. A great way to do this is by praying in tongues—*in* the Spirit. As you pray in tongues, you are praying the perfect will of God. Your mind is unfruitful, but your spirit is praying in agreement with the will of God. You can also pray in the Spirit in your native language. Paul wrote,

For if I pray in a tongue, my spirit prays, but my understanding is unfruitful. What is the conclusion then? I will pray with the spirit, and I will also pray with the understanding (1 Corinthians 14:14–15).

If you know that God has someone He wants you to pray for, spend some time praying in the Spirit before you meet with that person. Pray in tongues. Build up and edify your spirit, so that when you come into contact with this person for prayer, your natural words release supernatural power. Paul talks about praying with both the spirit and the understanding. Praying in tongues will infuse your words of understanding with supernatural power and give you a greater sensitivity as you are ministering healing to people.

Day Fourteen

STEP FOUR: REINTERVIEW AND CONTINUE PRAYING FOR EFFECT

One of the most important things about the reinterview process is the ability to see what God is doing. In this step, you will draw one of two conclusions: 1) Nothing is happening yet, or 2) something is happening. Today, I want to help you respond when *something* is happening, since the *Power to Heal* book shows you what to do when nothing seems to be happening.

Celebrate all signs of progress. If the person feels heat, that is good. If the person senses improvement, fantastic! If you notice some other kind of manifestation happening in the person—shaking, crying, trembling, laughing, etc.—then you need to celebrate. For the person who is either an unbeliever, or a Christian who does not necessarily believe in this kind of phenomena, the experience may be strange. They might try to resist it, feeling uncomfortable. Encourage them to receive what God is doing. Remind them that when God Almighty touches a human being, a reaction is going to take place. This is profoundly biblical. It is not the time to do a Bible study, but it is a time to remind the person you are praying for that the touch of the Holy Spirit brings results. The signs or manifestations they are experiencing indicate that God is up to something.

Create an atmosphere of thanksgiving. Recognize what God is doing and thank Him out loud for His power. This stirs up faith, both in you and in the person you are praying for. Learn to look for what God is doing every time you pray for someone. Any improvement is cause for thanksgiving. Every sign of God's presence and power touching that person is reason to celebrate. When you focus on what God *is* doing and honor it, you raise the faith level. The more faith you have, typically, the more healing happens.

ACTIVATE—LEARN HOW TO RECOGNIZE AND CELEBRATE WHAT GOD IS DOING

When you are praying for the sick, try to pay careful attention to how God is touching the person. As you reinterview him or her, ask questions that help people recognize what God is doing rather than what He is not doing.

- What are you feeling right now? Heat or warmth? Electricity? Anything unusual? (This is asked specifically in the area that needs healing.)

- Do you feel anything different in your body?

- Test out the part of your body that was in pain. Do you notice any results?

People have this idea that either healing happens instantly, or not at all—it is very black and white. Either someone lays hands on you and immediately you fall down and get healed, or nothing happens at all. This is a myth you need to help navigate people through. Healing can often be a process. For increased results, we often need increased faith. For this faith to rise up, learn the value of celebrating the healing progress that is happening rather than being discouraged by what has *not* happened yet.

Day Fifteen

STEP FIVE: POST PRAYER SUGGESTIONS

Keep on asking and it will be given you; keep on seeking and you will find;
keep on knocking [reverently] and [the door] will be opened to you.
MATTHEW 7:7 AMP

Perhaps one of the most important truths to share with people you pray with is the necessity of perseverance. Encourage the person to get prayer from others if there is little or no evidence of healing. Encourage them to persevere in prayer if their healing is partial and has not yet fully manifested. Encourage people to come back again for additional prayer. Remind them that sometimes healing is a process, and sometimes it occurs only after a number of prayers for healing have been made. Your job is to pray for healing and God's job is to heal the sick.

ACTIVATE—PERSEVERE TO EXPERIENCE GOD'S HEALING PROMISES

Read Luke 18:1–8, which is the parable of the persistent widow. Be encouraged to know that your God is not an *unjust judge*. If the judge in this parable was willing to respond to the widow's persistence, how much more is God willing to respond to the cries of His elect?

When you minister healing to an individual, and healing does not come or it comes partially, you must encourage perseverance. It is an essential biblical truth and a key to receiving from God. Remind the person of these truths about persevering in prayer:

- You are not trying to convince God to do something; the Bible reveals that His will is to heal.

- You are not begging God for your healing; you are acknowledging that you receive what Jesus has made available through the cross and desire to step into the fullness of His healing power.

- You are not asking God over and over again for the same thing, as if He didn't fully hear your request for healing the first time.

Perseverance is best understood as standing on God's healing promises and refusing to give up, no matter what the circumstances tell you. His promises are sure and steadfast.

SESSION 4

TESTIFY

SHARE MIRACLE STORIES THAT
CREATE AN ATMOSPHERE OF FAITH

Just like a salvation testimony has the ability to charge an atmosphere with faith for salvation, miracle testimonies infuse an atmosphere with faith for healing. Healing and miracle stories remind people that the same God who healed then can heal again today. Jesus is eternally unchanging and no respecter of persons. If He healed one person, He will do it for another!

For the testimony of Jesus is the spirit of prophecy.
—REVELATION 19:10

SESSION 4 SUMMARY

We need to combine prayer and testimony in order to have the greatest impact in the pursuit of healing. This session comes right after the five-step prayer model for good reason. In the actual video session, I simply share testimonies of how I have watched God's power in action.

Today, you are going to have a much more interactive group/class session. This is not simply a topic that you study; it is one that you put into practice. Testimonies release power and build faith as they are shared. We were never meant to simply keep the stories of God's mighty acts to ourselves. Throughout the Bible, we are constantly told to remember and to tell. We are to remember what God has done and we are to tell of His mighty acts. This includes everything from the supernatural work of salvation to the healing miracles He releases to us and through us.

DISCUSSION QUESTIONS

1. How did the stories that Randy shared in this session build up your faith? Which one(s) stood out to you?

2. Read Psalm 77:11, Psalm 105:5, and Psalm 143:5. What do all of these passages of Scripture have in common? What are they asking you to do?

3. Discuss some practical ways you can remember the works of God in your everyday life.

4. Do you have a system for keeping track of God's mighty works? If so, share it with the group/class.

5. Read Psalm 118:17 and Psalm 73:28. What do these verses of Scripture encourage you to do once you remember what God has done?

6. Why do think it is important for you to share your testimony in order for it to release faith-building power?

Transition to the group activation exercise. It is time to take what you just discussed and put it into practice.

GROUP ACTIVATION EXERCISE

Use this opportunity to have different people in the group or class come up and share testimonies of God's miracle-working power. (Preferably, these would be personal testimonies of how God healed them. For those people who do not have such testimonies, encourage them to tell other stories of people they personally know who have been healed.)

As you share testimonies of what God has done in your life, watch how this creates an atmosphere of faith. Be sensitive to how the Holy Spirit is moving among the group or class. As you sense the corporate level of faith increase, have people start praying for each other.

WEEKLY READING ASSIGNMENT

Be sure to read Chapters 10–12 in *Power to Heal* this week and complete your study guide assignments. This week is designed to help you reorient your thinking about the testimony. The exercises will take you through the process of remembering the works of God in your own life, studying them, and learning how these stories contain the power to release hope to others.

SESSION NOTES

CLAIM THE TESTIMONY

I have inherited Your testimonies forever, for they are the joy of my heart.
—**Psalm 119:111 NASB**

Y‌ou might think you are disqualified from this aspect of supernatural ministry because you personally do not have a healing testimony to share. Again, God has removed every barrier preventing your disqualification! You may not have a healing story, but I do. Take mine. Take the stories I talk about in the *Power to Heal* and on the DVDs. Claim these as your own. If you are praying for someone, feel free to share one of my stories from this book. They all accomplish the same goal—building faith to believe God for healing.

Use what you have access to. Draw from whatever well is available. Again, if you do have a personal healing testimony, or if you know someone who has been healed (like a family member or a friend), or you can remember a story from this study, *use it all.* Just be honest and authentic. I am not encouraging you to lie about it, replacing my name with yours. You do not need to pretend to be Randy Clark to be successful with this. It's not about my name or your name—it's about Jesus's name!

Trust the Holy Spirit to use these stories to build faith in those who need healing. At the day's end, whether you have a healing testimony or not, you actually have access to the *ultimate treasure of testimony*—Scripture. Every testimony in the Bible is your inheritance.

ACTIVATE—KEEP A WRITTEN RECORD OF TESTIMONIES

This week, I want to help you remember what God has done in and through you. I encourage you to purchase a journal or create a document where can you keep track of testimonies of God's healing, provision, and miraculous intervention in your life.

What is the purpose of this activation? So many people set out to journal with the most noble of intentions. We often fail in continuing such practices because we do not have a clear vision for the *why*. There is a very clear *why* that motivates us to keep a written record of testimonies.

Scripture tells us to study and meditate upon the *works* of God (we will look into this more thoroughly tomorrow). We are familiar with the concept of studying the Bible and meditating on God's Word, but to engage His works with the same amount of serious, diligent focus, we must start keeping a written record of these mighty exploits and supernatural deeds.

Make the works of God easy to reference in your life. When you have easy access to stories of His healing, miracle-working power, you are able to quickly reflect on what God has done in your life. You have instant access to the material God actually wants you to become a student of.

SAMPLE TESTIMONY JOURNAL ENTRY

You may not have a journal handy right now. That is okay. I want to remove every excuse for you not writing down the works of God. Take this moment to think about a time where God miraculously intervened in your life. For our purpose here, try to think of a *healing* testimony. If you personally do not have a healing testimony, think about someone you know who did receive miraculous healing through prayer. Write down the story below, recalling the details to the best of your ability.

BE HONEST IN RECORDING (AND SHARING) TESTIMONY

∼

I took my troubles to the Lord; I cried out to Him, and He answered my prayer.
—Psalm 120:1 NLT.

The psalmists are transparent in recounting the testimony of God's work in their lives. Time after time, we see a radical transition of circumstances. One minute David is in a pit of despair; the next his feet are planted on a rock. One moment the psalmist is bombarded by trouble and tribulation; the next he calls out to the Lord and his prayer is answered. Perhaps one of the great examples of this is Jonah. In the stomach of the great fish, the prophet said, *"I cried out to the Lord because of my affliction, and He answered me. Out of the belly of Sheol I cried, and You heard my voice"* (Jonah 2:2).

Take this opportunity to revisit the testimony that you wrote down yesterday. It is essential that in writing down our testimonies—and later on, sharing them—we are honest. Your honesty in accurately sharing the testimony can either bring someone into a place of breakthrough or discourage them right out of it.

If you were deathly ill, there seemed to be no hope you would get better, and then God supernaturally healed you, do *not* give people the impression that you have some enormous level of faith if you were getting ready to die. Be honest about your own healing journey and how God intervened, even if you did not expect it. Likewise, if you prayed for someone at one point, and you didn't have any faith for this person to be healed—and they still got healed—don't try to sugarcoat the story. Don't say that you had "mountain-moving" faith when you were really thinking to yourself, "God, I have no idea how this is going to happen." Be honest about your fears, thoughts, and your lack of faith—either in receiving healing for yourself or in praying for someone else. These stories are very revealing about the nature of the God who is faithful, even when we seem to be faithless. He still uses us to bring His healing power, even when we feel like we have absolutely no faith in that moment.

The other extreme is hyper-modesty. Don't act like you didn't have *any* faith for healing if you were actually very confident that God was going to come through and heal you or the person you were praying for. This tells people it is possible to experience that kind of supernatural confidence—faith that is absolutely convinced healing is imminent.

Both kinds of testimonies reveal that with God anything is possible. It is possible to have no faith, or very little faith, and still be healed. It is also possible to receive a supernatural deposit of extreme faith where you are absolutely, 100 percent convinced that you, or the person you are praying for, will be healed.

ACTIVATE—WRITE DOWN TWO HEALING TESTIMONIES—ONE OF HEALING RECEIVED AND THE OTHER OF HEALING RELEASED

I am going to give you another sample testimony journal page. Today, I want you to write down two healing testimonies:

1) Healing received. This is where you or someone else received healing from the Lord. Be honest in sharing this testimony. Specifically note what kind of faith you or the person had as you or they received healing.

2) Healing released. If you have prayed for the sick and seen them healed, write down your story of releasing God's healing power to someone else. What level of faith were you at when you witnessed the healing? If you do not have a story like this, try to find someone else who does. It is important for you to make these stories easily accessible and quickly referable.

TESTIMONY JOURNAL ENTRIES

Healing Received:

_____

_____

_____

_____

_____

_____

_____

_____

_____

_____

_____

_____

_____

_____

_____

_____

_____

_____

_____

Healing Released:

STUDY THE WORKS OF GOD

Great are the works of the Lord, studied by all who delight in them.
—PSALM 111:2 ESV

Today, I want to give you a clearer understanding of the *why* behind keeping a written record of the testimony. It's one thing to step out and start doing something. We start things all of the time. To maintain consistency in a practice, however, we constantly keep the end-result before us. You keep a written record of God's works so you can study them. Studying the testimony supernaturally reorients the way you think. You begin to think like God, and, as you do, you approach every opportunity to minister healing with increased confidence and greater effectiveness.

When it comes to teaching, we are familiar with how to study. In school, our teachers taught us information and asked us to study it. We studied what they taught so we could succeed on tests and ultimately pass our classes. Studying was instrumental in taking us to the next grade levels. This is certainly true for those of us who have gone to seminary or Bible school of some kind. Once again, we study certain academic and theological information for the purpose of expressing our intellectual mastery of the concepts we learned. This is helpful to succeed on tests and papers.

Now I want to introduce you to a different kind of studying that empowers you to succeed in healing and supernatural ministry. As you study testimonies, you are pondering them. You are reviewing what those stories say about who God is and what He will do. Studying the testimony actually brings you into new levels of faith and expectation. The miracle stories of God set a precedent. Testimonies orient your mind to instantly remember what God has done in the past. When you know what He has done, you can approach healing ministry with greater confidence. This is because what He has done, He will do again!

ACTIVATE—BECOME A STUDENT OF THE TESTIMONY

Review the testimonies you wrote down yesterday. Write down what these stories say about God's nature and His desire to heal. What do you learn about God from studying these testimonies?

TESTIMONY JOURNAL ENTRIES

Healing Received:

_____

_____

_____

_____

_____

_____

_____

_____

_____

_____

_____

_____

_____

_____

_____

_____

_____

Healing Released:

Day Nineteen

TESTIMONIES RELEASE PRAISE

~~~

Give ear, O my people, to my law; incline your ears to the words of my mouth.
I will open my mouth in a parable; I will utter dark sayings of old, which
we have heard and known, and our fathers have told us. We will not hide
them from their children, telling to the generation to come the praises of the
Lord, and His strength and His wonderful works that He has done.
—Psalm 78:1–4

These last two segments will be more interactive than informative. I want you to refer back to the two testimonies you wrote down a few days back, and study them with some specific results in mind. Just like we study information to pass a final exam, I want you to study those two testimonies motivated by a clear intention.

ACTIVATE—RELEASE PRAISE THROUGH THE TESTIMONY

Revisit your two healing testimonies and study them to see how they inspire praise. Revisit what God did and specifically write down the different reasons to praise God because of His healing power. Get detailed and specific here. Stretch yourself. Look for the attributes and characteristics of God that are revealed through your testimony.

In the same way that we study *hard* for a test, I encourage you to study just as vigorously to identify reasons to praise God in these accounts of testimony.

TESTIMONY JOURNAL ENTRIES

Healing Received: Reasons to Give God Praise

Healing Released: Reasons to Give God Praise

Healing Released: Reasons to Give God Praise

TESTIMONIES CREATE HOPE

For He established a testimony in Jacob, and appointed a law in Israel, which He commanded our fathers, that they should make them known to their children; that the generation to come might know them, the children who would be born, that they may arise and declare them to their children, that they may set their hope in God.
—PSALM 78:4–7

When you share testimony of God's healing power, it actually creates hope for people. For those who have been sick for years, your testimony might be the very thing that breaks them out of the prison of hopelessness. This is especially true for unbelievers and for Christians who do not know that God heals. If they are open and receptive to what you say, the words you share in the form of a story will expose them to a possibility they might have never considered before.

The God who healed you wants to also heal them. The God who healed *through you* desires to heal them using you as His vessel! Your testimony has the ability to awaken hope in the hopeless. This is why it is so important for you to share it accurately and honestly. God's power, in spite of your weakness, doubts, fears, or faithlessness, actually stirs up faith in people. If God could heal you in spite of your struggles, He can do the same for them!

ACTIVATE—CREATE HOPE BY SHARING TESTIMONY

Revisit your two healing testimonies and study them to see how they create hope. Revisit what God did and specifically write down the different ways that your stories can inspire hope in those who listen to them. Again, get detailed and specific. Stretch yourself. Look to see how your testimony gives people reasons to have hope.

TESTIMONY JOURNAL ENTRIES

Healing Received: Reason for Hope

Healing Released: Reason for Hope

_____

_____

_____

_____

_____

_____

_____

_____

_____

_____

_____

_____

_____

_____

_____

_____

_____

_____

_____

_____

_____

SESSION 5

THE AGONY OF DEFEAT

PERSEVERE THROUGH DEFEAT AND DISCOURAGEMENT

*It is absolutely wonderful to experience the thrill of victory in healing
ministry: the signs and wonders, the miracles, and the healings. Yet there is
a price to be paid for a person to press into a greater anointing for healing
ministry. We respond to defeat by learning to press ahead and persevere despite
the failures, disappointments, and pain that comes with healing ministry.*

~~~

*If anyone desires to come after Me, let him deny himself,
and take up his cross daily, and follow Me.*
—LUKE 9:23

SESSION 5 SUMMARY

The first four sessions of this study guide were designed to get you activated; the next four are essential foundations for *sustaining* a healing ministry in your life or church. Any Christian can step out, take risks, pray for the sick, and watch God start to heal people. This is because the Spirit of God lives inside of us and it is He who does the supernatural work through us.

However, once you find yourself praying for the sick for any length of time, you will discover that not everyone you pray for gets healed. Your commission is to pray; God's job is to heal. So many believers have given up on praying for the sick because of the defeat they have suffered in the process. Either they have seen too many people *not* healed or they have experienced personal loss themselves. In order to continue in the ministry of healing, it is vital to understand what it costs to persevere—this is the cross Jesus has called us to carry. This session on the agony of defeat shows you how to keep moving forward, even when you have experienced personal defeat and discouragement in praying for the sick.

DISCUSSION QUESTIONS

1. What were your thoughts about what Randy shared about the agony of defeat in regard to healing ministry?

2. What are some of the reasons that people do not practice healing ministry today?

3. What is the main reason that people do not pray for the sick today?

4. What is the cost or cross of the healing ministry?

5. Why do you think it is important to honestly talk through our defeats in healing ministry?

6. Why is it important to learn how to persevere through the agony of defeat if you want to continue to release God's healing power in your life?

7. How do you think this teaching can sustain you through discouragement and difficulty in praying for the sick?

8. In healing ministry, what is our responsibility and what is God's job?

GROUP ACTIVATION EXERCISE

This is a time to pray and receive encouragement from the Holy Spirit. Most likely, there are people in the group or class who have experienced discouragement in this area of praying for the sick. This tends to be the result of praying for a loved one who did not receive healing. This is not a time to single anyone out for personal ministry—this can take place after the class, if a person requests personal prayer. This is a time to encourage, refresh, and empower each other to keep pressing in when praying for the sick.

WEEKLY READING ASSIGNMENT

Be sure to read Chapters 13–15 in *Power to Heal* this week and complete your study guide assignments.

SESSION NOTES

HEALING MINISTRY IS COSTLY

*If anyone desires to come after Me, let him deny himself,
and take up his cross daily, and follow Me.*
—LUKE 9:23

Our culture has done everything possible to strip the cross of its weightiness by placing it on jewelry or using it as an icon to adorn church steeples. Crosses are everywhere in our twenty-first-century culture. Perhaps this is one of the reasons so many are ill-equipped to "take up their cross daily." They have no clear idea of what this looks like. The cross is just something else we put on; it's an addition to what we already have. We have become too familiar and comfortable with the cross. Rewind to the context of Luke 9 and you will be sure to discover how uncomfortable Jesus's audience was with the words that He was sharing. The cross was not an "add-on" to them. Rather, this object was understood as an object of suffering.

Jesus's disciples knew that to "take up a cross" meant to experience personal suffering. Here is the reality for us today—the same cross that testified of incredible suffering also represents the ministry of healing. It costs to take up the cross of healing because we will experience uncomfortable, painful suffering. It is unfortunate that we see taking up this cross as optional. It is not at all optional if we truly want to follow Jesus and be His disciples.

To exclusively preach His power without the fellowship of His suffering is incorrect theology. There is suffering that comes with the healing ministry. However, on the other side of suffering is tremendous victory. There are those who will not be healed, and we need to learn to persevere through that. We need to be okay with saying, "I don't know," and not trying to come up with a theological excuse. Remember, our commission is to pray for the sick and God's job is to heal. If the healing doesn't happen, it does not mean God has changed. He is unchanging. He was, is, and forever will be the Healer. This is where mystery comes into the picture. This is why "I don't know" is such a liberating response. Embrace the cost. Yes, healing ministry comes with great suffering and pain. It also brings some of the most exhilarating, thrilling victories you will ever experience.

DISCUSSION QUESTIONS

1. How is healing ministry costly? Have you ever thought about it in these terms, relating it to the cross of Luke 9:23?

_____

_____

_____

_____

_____

_____

_____

_____

_____

_____

2. In what ways do you think perseverance is important in order to continue in the healing ministry?

_____

_____

_____

_____

_____

_____

_____

_____

_____

YOU HAVE BEEN COMMISSIONED TO HEAL THE SICK!

Go into all the world and preach the gospel to every creature. He who believes and is baptized will be saved; but he who does not believe will be condemned. And these signs will follow those who believe…they will lay hands on the sick, and they will recover.
—MARK 16:15–16,18

There are many different reasons people throughout the ages have not participated in healing ministry. You heard about some of these in the video sessions. To think about healing in terms of something we can "take or leave" is missing the point completely. The Great Commission lists healing as a key component. In Matthew 28, Jesus tells the disciples to teach others the same things they were taught by Him. What did Jesus both teach and show the disciples? Of the many things, one of them was how to heal the sick.

When we believe the healing ministry is optional, it becomes easier for us to give up, especially when we encounter defeat. However, when we go back to the black and white instructions of Jesus, we are challenged by the nonnegotiable nature of healing ministry. It truly is for all believers—not just holy people of old who became canonized as saints. It is not just for bishops, elders, pastors, or religious leaders. Not just the notable healing evangelists. And it is not just for the early church, the apostles, or Jesus. Healing is a key component of the Great Commission. It releases the Kingdom of God among humankind and demonstrates the absolute supremacy of Jesus over all things.

Yes, there will be disappointment in healing ministry. However, you also experience disappointment when sharing your faith. Not everyone you talk to about Jesus makes an immediate profession of faith. This reality does not discourage the church from giving up on evangelism. Let's approach healing the same way. Just because there is discouragement, this does not give us license to reject a vital ministry that was modeled by Jesus Himself.

REFLECTION QUESTIONS

1. Why do you think someone would consider healing as a "take it or leave it" ministry and not an essential part of Christian discipleship?

2. Based on the teaching you have heard in the video session and read in Power to Heal, describe why healing the sick is an important ministry for you to be involved in today. (Remember, it's only when you understand its importance that you will continue to pray for the sick, even when you experience defeat.)

PREACH THE WORD, NOT YOUR EXPERIENCE

Proclaim the message; be persistent whether the time is favorable or unfavorable.
—2 TIMOTHY 4:2 NRSV

Our experience cannot determine our theology. If this happens, God is always changing. And if God is always changing, the danger is that a changing God is not the God of Scripture. Rather, a changing "god" is a deity we have fashioned in our own image, based on personal experience. This is a subtle form of idolatry that has crept into the church and distracted so many believers from faithfully sharing the truth of God's Word, regardless of whether their experience has caught up to it yet.

There are certain principles in the Bible that, yes, we must preach out of experience. Let me put it this way—it is better for us to draw from our history of experience when presenting those principles. A single, twenty-year-old pastor giving advice about marriage and raising a family just does not have a lot of substance behind it. Can he still share about such things? Yes, but it does not carry as much weight as a more seasoned leader who is both a husband and father. This is one valid expression of preaching out of experience.

Let's transition to the supernatural now. There are realities that Jesus has invited all believers to participate in. The problem is that we shy away from pressing into these truths because of our present level of experience. In Matthew 10:8, Jesus instructs the disciples, *"Heal the sick, raise the dead, cleanse those who have leprosy, drive out demons. Freely you have received; freely give."* At one point, the disciples had never participated in supernatural ministry. It was all new to them. Perhaps this was their first commission of this kind, perhaps not. Either way, we have to assume by default that there was a first time that Jesus sent them out to heal the sick and they were not experienced. Their experience was at one level, but the words of Jesus invited them into another.

How did they respond? They listened and went. And as they went, they healed. They faithfully and persistently proclaimed the message, whether the time was *"favorable or unfavorable."* At least at one point, I can assure you, the time was unfavorable. I'm sure the first time they heard Jesus invite them to heal the sick or raise the dead, they thought, "Wait a minute, Jesus…were You calling *me* to do this? I thought this was only stuff that *You* did. After all, *You* are Jesus."

Jesus invited the disciples to elevate their level of experience to align with His Word. He is doing the same for us today. Don't define Jesus or attempt to understand His works through your lens of personal experience. Those experiences include loss, failure, defeat, and disappointment. We cannot make theological conclusions about God based on our experiences of failure. His Word is our final standard, and it is only this that should set our expectation.

REFLECTION QUESTIONS

1. Are there areas where you have changed the way you see God because of your personal experiences (defeats, discouragements, losses, disappointments, etc.)?

2. How are these truths calling you higher when it comes to having a correct view of God and healing ministry?

_____

_____

_____

_____

_____

_____

_____

_____

_____

_____

_____

_____

_____

ACTIVATE

I want you to press in to see your experience agree with the truth of God. Pray that the Holy Spirit would strengthen you to persist past your defeats and continue to pray for the sick.

You don't have to pretend the defeats didn't happen, nor do you need to have an explanation—"I don't know" is sufficient. All you need to do is remember who God is based on the eternal standard of His Word. He is unchanging. He is the same yesterday, today, and forever. Don't bring God down to your level of experience. If anything, He is calling you upward. He is inviting you into His level of experience.

THE DUAL REALITIES OF DEFEAT AND VICTORY

Keep on asking, and you will receive what you ask for. Keep on seeking, and
you will find. Keep on knocking, and the door will be opened to you.
—MATTHEW 7:7 NLT

Don't let defeat stop you from pressing in. Don't let discouragement keep you persevering for victory. The principle of Matthew 7:7 is very applicable to continuing in the healing ministry. Jesus is calling us into a stalwart, immovable stance. He doesn't say, "Ask, but then stop asking when you experience defeat," or "Ask, but stop asking when what you asked for doesn't happen." He simply invites us to continue asking.

Here is a fact: You cannot have victory without defeat in healing ministry. After over twenty years of healing ministry, I have seen some incredible victories. That said, I have also deeply experienced the agony of defeat. In the *Power to Heal*, I share several stories—many of which occurred over a six-month period—and they are all painful. We cannot allow defeat to stop us from praying, or else we will not experience any victories. This is how defeat and victory go hand in hand. For us to continue in the healing ministry, we need to engage it realistically.

If defeat causes you to stop praying for the sick, by default you will never experience the thrill of victory. While God is known to sovereignly heal people, be it in His presence or through some other kind of supernatural experience, His primary method for releasing healing is through Spirit-filled vessels. Our hands are catalysts that release God's healing power. Our words carry the weight and power of the Kingdom of God. It has nothing to do with us; it has everything to do with the Spirit inside of us and the Word of God in our mouths. For us to step back from the ministry of healing, we are actually depriving the sick of hope for wholeness. This is all part of the cross of the healing ministry.

The only other option is to embrace a counterfeit, painless cross that costs us nothing. Many have done this, and, as a result, have embraced a Christian life that is subpar to what Jesus made available. This is not a heaven or hell question by any means. In fact, some of these people are incredibly godly. They walk in holiness, are radically devoted to Jesus, and exhibit the fruit of the Spirit in their lives. Just imagine the level of increased effectiveness they would walk in *if* they continued to carry the cross of the healing ministry. Don't let this be you. Continue onward. Defeat is not an invitation to give up; it's a summons to keep pressing, asking, praying, and believing.

REFLECTION QUESTIONS

1. What does the following statement mean to you: If defeat stops you from praying for the sick, you will never get to experience healing victories?

2. Why do you think it's so important for Christians to embrace a healing ministry that involves both victory and defeat? What happens if we don't factor in the defeats when we start praying for the sick?

TWO REQUIREMENTS TO EMBRACING SUFFERING IN HEALING MINISTRY

I want to know Christ—yes, to know the power of His resur-
rection and participation in His sufferings..
—PHILIPPIANS 3:10 NIV

To pray for the sick, we must recognize that there is a high emotional price tag that comes along with it. Christianity has become too comfortable. Any thought of suffering, or even dealing with people who are experiencing suffering, is off-putting to us. We must persevere through this mentality. Praying for the sick deeply touches your heart. It also puts you in a place where God is not optional. You need His power, yes, to bring healing, but you also need it to persevere. You need supernatural grace to keep going when you don't see results, or worse, when the results have been discouraging.

Sometimes, you will feel like you can't go on because it's too much to bear. Don't be mistaken—the healing ministry is one of the most difficult ministries that you could ever have. You must be ready to handle failure. You must be willing to say, "I don't know," when people don't get healed. Why did this person get healed and that one didn't? "I don't know." Why did that sinner get healed while that pillar in the church died of the same condition? "I don't know."

To be involved in the healing ministry, you must be willing to embrace emotional suffering and be willing to say, "I don't know." These are the two critical requirements. Are you willing? The more who say yes to this cross, the more we will see the power of God demonstrated in our day like never before.

REFLECTION QUESTIONS

1. Read Philippians 3:10 and consider how this Scripture specifically relates to the healing ministry.

_____

_____

_____

_____

_____

_____

_____

_____

2. Have you personally suffered the agony of defeat in healing ministry? How has this impacted the way you pray today?

_____

_____

_____

_____

_____

_____

_____

_____

Take this opportunity to talk through your discouragement and defeat with the Holy Spirit. Let Him bring healing to your heart. Ask Him to strengthen you to persevere in this ministry, even though it is costly. Finally, ask Him to give you a vision of a reward that is worthy of the cost. The reward is seeing the sick healed, hopeless situations supernaturally transformed, and the name of Jesus being wonderfully exalted in the earth.

SESSION 6

THE THRILL OF VICTORY

HEALING'S RELATIONSHIP TO THE GRACE OF GOD

These five healing principles are true, but at the same time,
can be supernaturally overridden.
Never forget that God's grace is often greater than
the healing principles we come up with.

Jesus Christ is the same yesterday, today, and forever.
—HEBREWS 13:8

SESSION 6 SUMMARY

Jesus Christ is the same yesterday, today and forever. His character and nature are eternally unchanging. He is the Healer. This defines a foundational aspect of God's personality. Even though His character does not change, the ways that He releases healing do vary from time to time and from case to case. The five principles that I discuss in this session are not designed to become iron-clad laws. They are grace guideposts purposed to help you recognize different ways that God moves and heals. Scripture clearly shows how each of these five principles can release the thrill of victory. At the same time, God is bigger than the principles we try to build around Him.

You will notice each of these five principles visibly at work in Scripture and present in the Kingdom today as God demonstrates His healing power. It is important to recognize how God is moving. Instead of trying to get God to heal on our terms, we turn our attention toward His work and participate with what the Holy Spirit is doing. This is why these five principles are so foundational. Even though God is known to violate them, He is also faithful to consistently uphold them.

DISCUSSION QUESTIONS/GROUP ACTIVATION EXERCISE

The goal of the questions in this particular session is to incite discussion and, most importantly, to build faith through shared testimony. This should be the end-result of the activation exercise: the group/class is to be built up in their faith and stirred afresh to pray for healing because they were encouraged by the stories of their peers experiencing the thrill of victory.

1. Why is it important for us not to turn these five principles into laws? Discuss each of the five principles and how group/class members have actually seen these at work in their lives. Encourage them to share testimonies.

2. Why is faith so important for healing?

    a. Can you share a testimony where you had strong faith to believe for healing and it happened?

    b. Can you share a testimony where you had *no* faith for healing (or the person you prayed for didn't have any faith for healing), and God still healed?

3. How can sin prevent healing?

    a. Have you ever been in a situation where you had to help lead someone through the process of repenting of sin, and then saw healing take place? Explain.

    b. How has God healed people who *had* sin in their lives? Did the healing bring them to a place of repentance?

4. How does God work through specific anointed people? Share a testimony when God used an "anointed person" to bring healing in your life (or in the life of someone you know).

5. In what ways have you felt the anointing?

    a. Share about a time where you physically felt the anointing, prayed for the sick, and saw healing take place?

    b. Share about a time where you felt absolutely *nothing* and were still used by God to release His healing power?

6. Why is compassion so important for healing ministry?

    a. Share about how God moved you through compassion to pray for healing and you watched someone get healed.

    b. You can also share about a time where you felt like you had *no* compassion, but prayed for healing anyway, and God demonstrated His compassion *through* you to heal someone.

WEEKLY READING ASSIGNMENT

Be sure to read Chapters 16–17 in *Power to Heal* this week and complete your study guide assignments.

SESSION NOTES

THE PRINCIPLE OF FAITH

Have faith in God. For assuredly, I say to you, whoever says to this mountain, "Be removed and be cast into the sea," and does not doubt in his heart, but believes that those things he says will be done, he will have whatever he says. Therefore I say to you, whatever things you ask when you pray, believe that you receive them, and you will have them.
—MARK 11:22–24

Where there is more faith, more happens. It's just that simple. This is one of the key reasons we create an atmosphere of faith by sharing testimonies and stories of God's power. I do this routinely, either through sharing about them myself, bringing the actual people up to tell their stories, or playing videos that show the actual miracle in action. Testimonies release faith and create an atmosphere where people more easily believe for healing.

In Mark 11:22–24, Jesus gives us a very simple faith reality. Sometimes we have difficulty with this Scripture. In this case, it is not that the verse is so obscure—these passages are as plain as day. The real problem is coming to walk in the reality of what this Scripture reveals. The challenge before the church is not understanding something difficult, but walking in light of the truth of truths that are really clear and plain.

Jesus is extending an invitation and a promise to us in this passage. It is supernatural, and it is outside the realm of possibility. He is challenging us to see and live on a higher level, and this is why people try to take Bible passages that speak of the supernatural and naturalize them. We want something comfortable, not demanding. The faith that Jesus describes is demanding. It confronts us with our present condition and calls us up higher.

ACTIVATE—MORE FAITH MEANS MORE HAPPENS—FIND PRACTICAL WAYS TO KEEP YOUR FAITH STRONG

What are some practical ways you can keep your faith strong? (Finding and studying testimonies is one example.)

_____

_____

_____

_____

_____

_____

_____

_____

_____

_____

_____

_____

_____

_____

_____

_____

_____

_____

_____

SIN BLOCKING THE FLOW OF HEALING

〜

Later Jesus found him at the temple and said to him, "See, you are well
again. Stop sinning or something worse may happen to you".
—JOHN 5:14 NIV

Sin can be related to sickness. Sickness is not necessarily evidence of God smiting someone for his or her sinful choices or lifestyle; instead, it is often the consequence of a choice of the person who sinned.

In Mark 2, we read about the man who was paralyzed, whose four friends brought him to Jesus. Since they could not press through the crowd, they ultimately climbed up to the roof, broke through the ceiling, and lowered their paralyzed friend down to where Jesus was. Jesus, seeing the man, said, *"Son, your sins are forgiven you"* (Mark 2:5).

The Pharisees got upset because only God could forgive sin, and for Jesus to make a statement absolving this man of sin was, in effect, declaring Himself to be God. They thought such a statement was blasphemy, which it was—unless it was true. Jesus looked at them and said, *"Why do you reason about these things in your hearts? Which is easier, to say to the paralytic, 'Your sins are forgiven you,' or to say, 'Arise, take up your bed and walk'? But that you may know that the Son of Man has power on earth to forgive sins"*—He said to the paralytic, *"I say to you, arise, take up your bed, and go to your house"* (Mark 2:8–11). That is exactly what happened. We see that *"immediately he arose, took up the bed, and went out in the presence of them all, so that all were amazed and glorified God"* (Mark 2:12).

What was the first thing that Jesus said to this paralyzed man? *"Son, your sins are forgiven."* Some diseases and sicknesses are actually related to sin. The key word here is "some." This is not all encompassing for all matters of sickness and disease. Also, you should never allow someone's sin or sinful lifestyle to prevent you from praying for healing.

ACTIVATE—SIN CAN CAUSE SICKNESS, BUT IT SHOULD NEVER PREVENT YOU FROM PRAYING FOR HEALING

If you are praying for someone—and there is sin in his or her life—what are some appropriate responses you might have? (You might want to refer to the chapter "Five-step Prayer Model" in *Power to Heal*.) Write some of these out in the space provided.

THE PRINCIPLE OF THE ANOINTED PERSON

...to another gifts of healings by the same Spirit.
—1 CORINTHIANS 12:7

All believers have been commissioned to pray for the sick. With that in mind, you will also note that there have been some unique cases of people who seemed especially anointed to heal the sick. God used them as vessels for the gift of healing, as described in 1 Corinthians 12:7. With that said, any Christian can receive a gift of healing at any time, as the Spirit gives gifts as He wills to whomever He so chooses at anytime He wants.

There have been anointed individuals like Kathryn Kuhlman, Oral Roberts, and other evangelists who have had powerful ministries of healing. I honor them. Even though these people have witnessed incredible victories in healing, they have also experienced the agony of defeat. Just because someone is not healed under a certain person's ministry does not give us the right to denounce the healing evangelist as false or phony. He or she is simply human. These evangelists have to navigate through defeat in the same way that you and I do. Likewise, God has used and continues to use such individuals in a powerful way to bring healing to the sick.

With that said, I have never believed that God could *only* use these "men and women of power for the hour." I have always believed that all Christians have been graciously invited into the ministry of healing. We are all commissioned to pray for the sick. As one of my friends has said, the essence of my message can be summed up in one sentence: "More people get healed when more people pray for healing."

Remind yourself: God can use little ole me! You don't have to be the anointed man or woman of God to pray for the sick. You have the Holy Spirit living within you. You've received a commission from Jesus. Go forth, step out, take risks, and believe that God is with you to back up His Word!

ACTIVATE—GOD CAN USE ESPECIALLY ANOINTED MEN AND WOMEN TO HEAL THE SICK—HE CAN ALSO USE YOU BECAUSE YOU ARE ANOINTED

Describe what it means to be "anointed" by the Holy Spirit. Also, consider what this means for you as you pray for the sick. Yes, there have been and continue to be people who are especially anointed for healing ministry. These are unusual cases and they should not keep you from praying for the sick, desiring the same results. Write out your thoughts in the space below.

THE PRINCIPLE OF FEELING THE ANOINTING

Immediately the fountain of her blood was dried up, and she felt in her body that she was healed of the affliction. And Jesus, immediately knowing in Himself that power had gone out of Him, turned around in the crowd and said, "Who touched My clothes?"
—MARK 5:29–30

Jesus actually felt power go out of Him as this woman touched the hem of His garment. Likewise, there will be times as you are praying for people when you will physically feel something take place. You might be praying for the person and, all of a sudden, feel a surge of power. You may feel heat or electricity on your hands. Respond to what the Holy Spirit seems to be doing at those times. These are signs to you that are intended to build your faith for healing.

It is interesting because it is common for the people you pray for to feel such sensations or experience these manifestations. God starts to touch them physically and they describe a physical reaction taking place. Often, though, the person doing the praying feels nothing. This is why faith is such a significant part of the healing ministry. I know this is true for me. By and large, I do not usually feel anything as I pray for healing. The people I pray for often experience some kind of sensation, but the majority of what I do involves faith and obedience. I just do what I know He wants me to do, participating with the Holy Spirit as I go through the process.

The bottom line is this: Whether you physically feel a sensation, or feel nothing at all, step out in faith. If you feel the anointing, wonderful—take it as God's cue for you to step out and believe for a miracle. If you feel nothing, fantastic—take it as God's cue for you to step out and believe for a miracle. Admittedly, the feeling does *increase* or *build* your faith. Still, you have the same faith inside of you. Whether you feel the anointing or not, step out. Take the risk and believe that God wants to release His power through you.

ACTIVATE—WHILE PRAYING FOR THE SICK, YOU MAY FEEL THE ANOINTING—BE SURE TO RESPOND TO WHAT GOD IS DOING

If you start to feel some kind of physical sensation while praying for the sick, how should you respond?

Day Thirty

COMPASSION

⌇

And when Jesus went out He saw a great multitude; and He was
moved with compassion for them, and healed their sick.
—MATTHEW 14:14

Scripture shows us how Jesus was moved by compassion and healed the sick. If faith is the greatest principle of all, this one is the next greatest—moving with compassion. Follow your heart. Many of the healings that I have seen are directed to somebody just by a tug of the heart. I don't know why, but when you begin to talk to somebody and find out they have a certain problem or condition, you find yourself wanting to pray for them. You are moved toward that person because of the compassion of Christ operating in you and through you.

Healing is not just about getting a certain result. There are those who actually pursue the ministry of healing with the wrong intentions. They are following formulas, not being moved by compassion. They want to see results, but they are not ultimately concerned about the people feeling loved and being made whole. We cannot get caught up in the alleged glamour of the healing ministry (although, after going through the agony of defeat, the glamour fades quickly). Yes, we celebrate the incredible miracles that our eyes get to behold. Of course our hearts are thrilled and excited as broken bodies are touched by the victory that Jesus purchased at Calvary and they receive healing.

Maybe the person got healed, maybe they didn't. At the end of a prayer session with you, do people feel loved? Do they feel like you have genuine compassion for their needs, or do they feel like you are turning them into a ministry project just to get a miracle? Let's make the great aim of healing ministry expressing the compassionate and loving nature of the Lord Jesus. He brings wholeness because He loves people. He healed in the Gospels because He was moved and motivated by a heart of compassion.

ACTIVATE—AS YOU PRAY FOR PEOPLE, MAKE YOUR HIGHEST AIM FOR THEM TO FEEL LOVED BY GOD

What are some practical ways that you can help people feel the compassion and love of God as you pray for their healing? Write down your thoughts below.

SESSION 7

WORDS OF KNOWLEDGE FOR HEALING

UNLOCK GOD'S PROPHETIC POWER

The anointing is not you just having an experience or a feeling; it is the empowerment to do something. When you receive a word of knowledge, you are flowing in the anointing to release the love and power of Jesus to someone else.

~

There are diversities of gifts, but the same Spirit. There are differences of ministries, but the same Lord. And there are diversities of activities, but it is the same God who works all in all. But the manifestation of the Spirit is given to each one for the profit of all: for to one is given the word of wisdom through the Spirit, to another the word of knowledge through the same Spirit.
—1 CORINTHIANS 12:4–8

SESSION 7 SUMMARY

Words of knowledge work hand in hand with healing. In this session, Randy shares about different ways you can receive words of knowledge.

DISCUSSION QUESTIONS/GROUP ACTIVATION EXERCISE

For this session, the discussion questions are going to be minimal since words of knowledge need to be practiced in order to be understood. Review some of the "ground rules" for words of knowledge before encouraging the group to begin sharing them.

1. What is a word of knowledge?

2. What is the purpose for sharing words of knowledge?

3. How do words of knowledge work together with healing?

4. What are some of the different ways you can receive a word of knowledge? Explain.

5. Share testimonies of how you have received words of knowledge for healing (and saw God heal because of those words)?

Ask for some volunteers to come up to the front of the group/class who will be willing to receive and call out words of knowledge. Next, take some time to pray. Pray as a group, praying in the Holy Spirit (tongues) if the group is comfortable doing so. Ask the Holy Spirit to come and reveal words of knowledge for healing.

Yes, this is a time of practice, but it is also an opportunity for the Holy Spirit to come in power and genuinely touch people. Be aware of this throughout the exercise. You can:

- Continue praying, encouraging the entire group or class to spend the next five to ten minutes in prayer (perhaps in separate places throughout the room).

- Encourage nonvolunteers that the Lord might give them words of knowledge as well—*be open and listening!*

- You could also play some light music in the background.

Have the volunteers spend time in prayer. Encourage them to be bold and unafraid of being wrong. It is a safe environment where they will not be judged. Ask them to write down the words of knowledge the Lord shares with them. After the time of prayer ends, have each volunteer come before the group and share their words of knowledge. Encourage the group/class members to respond immediately if they hear their conditions called out. Have the person receiving the word of knowledge pray for the person with the stated condition.

WEEKLY READING ASSIGNMENT—LEARN HOW TO RECEIVE WORDS OF KNOWLEDGE

Be sure to read Chapters 18–19 in *Power to Heal* this week and complete your study guide assignments. This week, your assignments are going to be very specific. *Power to Heal* and the curriculum session will give you a clearer idea of what a word of knowledge is.

Consider the five ways you might receive words of knowledge. Through different stories and teaching, you will receive a clear idea of five different ways God might give you a word. By the week's end, you should be a little more comfortable comfortable recognizing and sharing words of knowledge for healing.

SESSION NOTES

FEEL IT

I learned about "feeling" words of knowledge from my friend Edna. Edna was an American Baptist who had been to seminary and happened to be charismatic. She and I were talking one day and I asked her if she received words of knowledge. "Yes," she replied, and then went on to tell me that she felt them in her body. "You check your body out before you go to church, and when you get to church, if you feel pain that is not yours, that's a word of knowledge," she said. Today, I receive 95 percent of my words of knowledge by feeling them. I literally feel the "word" in my body as a physical pain that I normally do not have.

ACTIVATE—LEARN HOW TO RECOGNIZE A "FELT" WORD OF KNOWLEDGE

Based on this description of *feeling* words of knowledge, describe what this experience might feel like to you. Have you ever had this happen? If so, explain.

READ IT

To *read* a word of knowledge, you literally see the words spelled out in front of you—you even sometimes see them on people. When you "read" a word of knowledge in this way you can actually see words moving across in front of you in your mind's eye. For some people, it's like a big newspaper headline going across in front of them, while other people see it like a stock-market ticker tape moving in front of their eyes. They can actually read the words.

I have never received a word of knowledge in this way before. However, I've talked with many people who have had them this way. It also seems that people who receive words in this way are very accurate when they give them.

A friend of mine who is gifted in the word of knowledge was praying for someone. He actually "saw" this person's medical chart. He didn't know what some of the terms were, but he saw and read the medical chart. Because my friend saw it and could read it, he could share with confidence some of the names of certain ailments that he had never heard of before. Reading a word like this, where you read someone's medical chart, will encourage faith in the person giving the word as well as the one receiving it. The more accurate the word, the more faith will rise in the hearts of everyone around to receive all that God has for them.

ACTIVATE—WHEN YOU SEE WORDS OF KNOWLEDGE SCROLLING IN FRONT OF YOUR EYES, SPEAK OUT WHAT YOU SEE

How does this expression of the word of knowledge build up faith in both the person who is sharing the word and the person who is receiving it? Write down your thoughts below.

_____

_____

_____

_____

SEE IT

In this case, you don't read it, but you see the word of knowledge like a picture in your mind. One night at a Presbyterian church, my wife, DeAnne, received a word of knowledge. She said, "Kidney." A little girl who had a kidney disorder came up, and we prayed for her. A few weeks later, the girl's healing was confirmed.

Knowing that my wife had no idea what a kidney looked like, I asked her on the way home how she got the word about the kidney.

"I saw it," she said.

"Well, how did you know it was a kidney?" I asked.

"I didn't," she said. "I saw something but didn't know what it was. I just saw this thing, and I asked, 'God, what is that?' And then the impression came—'kidney.'"

ACTIVATE—YOU MAY SEE IMAGES OR PICTURES THAT WILL BE WORDS OF KNOWLEDGE

How might God speak to you using images or pictures to give you a word of knowledge? Write down your thoughts below.

_____

_____

_____

_____

_____

_____

_____

Day Thirty-four

THINK IT

Ihave only had a few words of knowledge from thoughts or impressions. One notable instance was where I had a real sharp pain in my lower back. When I gave the word, a woman in our church by the name of Gail came up. Knowing she had responded to that word, I was watching her. As I watched, I received an impression. The Lord said, "Degeneration."

So I asked, "Gail, is your spinal problem due to degeneration of the spine?"

"Yes," she said.

"God is going to heal you!" I said.

I had a lot of faith about this. As we started to pray, she began to shake and to perspire. She fell forward onto the altar, trembling under the power of God's healing anointing for several minutes. When she went back to the doctor, they confirmed that she was completely healed by God's power!

You can think words of knowledge or get an impression in your mind or heart. In my experience, I would say that the two most common ways of receiving a word of knowledge are feeling them and thinking them.

ACTIVATE—GOD MIGHT PLACE AN IMPRESSION OR THOUGHT IN YOUR MIND THAT IS REALLY A WORD OF KNOWLEDGE

How would you go about recognizing whether the thought or impression is a word of knowledge from the Holy Spirit? Write down your thoughts below.

_____

_____

_____

_____

_____

Day Thirty-five

SAY IT

The fifth way to receive words of knowledge is what I used to call "automatic speech." However, because of the occult connotations with that term, it is not a good choice of words. I prefer to call it "inspired speech" instead.

This way tends to come abruptly while I'm praying or talking with someone. As I'm praying for them, I hear myself say something that I didn't mean or plan on saying. It is like speaking in tongues—it bypasses the cognitive part of the mind. It shocks me that I even say the word. I'll be praying for somebody and hear myself say, "And I pray that you'll forgive your brother who stole that forty dollars from you in 1930," or something weird like that. I'll wonder, "Where did that even come from?" Instantly tears will come to the person's eyes, and I know God has given them a word of knowledge.

You don't think about saying it; it just comes out of your mouth. You actually hear it for the first time yourself when you speak it out. Sometimes, you don't even recognize what you say. You just think that you're praying as you always would. But God speaks through you when you don't even know it. It bypasses the cognitive processes of the brain.

ACTIVATE—YOU MAY RECEIVE A WORD OF KNOWLEDGE WHILE YOU ARE PRAYING FOR SOMEONE OR SAYING SOMETHING

Most likely, you have experienced this expression of the word of knowledge. You end up praying for someone or talking to a person, and all of a sudden, you share something that, in your own natural mind, you had no way of knowing and weren't even thinking about.

When you receive words of knowledge in this manner, what is a good way to follow up with the person you spoke the word to? Write down your thoughts below.

SESSION 8

FAITH

FOUR KINDS OF FAITH THAT POSITION PEOPLE FOR HEALING

*When you know what level of faith a person is at, you are equipped
to pray for healing more specifically and effectively. Jesus never
rejected people because of their level of faith; He worked with them,
bringing them to a place where they could receive healing.*

~

Truly I tell you, if you have faith as small as a mustard seed, you can say to this mountain, "Move from here to there," and it will move. Nothing will be impossible for you.
—MATTHEW 17:20 NIV

SESSION 8 SUMMARY

It is important for you to know what kind of faith someone has so you can pray for them most effectively. After listening to Randy share about the four different stories from the book of Mark, you will quickly learn that God can work with any level of faith. Nothing is impossible or off limits to Him. However, as you participate with God in the healing ministry, it is helpful to know where someone is at in his or her faith so you can come alongside that person and work with that specific level of faith.

DISCUSSION QUESTIONS

1. Why do you think it's important to know where someone's faith level is at when you are praying for healing?

2. Describe "if you can" faith, which is based on the story of the father and his demonized son (see Mark 9:17–29).

a. What does this kind of faith look and sound like?

b. Have you ever experienced this level of faith when praying for the sick?

c. Has this ever described you?

3. Describe "if you are willing" faith, which is based on the story of the man with leprosy (see Mark 1:40–42).

a. Why is it so important to know that God is able *and* willing to heal?

b. What does Jesus's willingness reveal about God's desire to heal?

c. How does this level of faith prevent people from being expectant when it comes to receiving healing?

4. Describe "if I can" faith, which is based on the story of the woman with the issue of blood (see Mark 5:24–34).

a. How does this woman show her great faith?

b. What makes this level of faith different from "if you are willing" or "if you can" faith?

c. How is great faith expressed and demonstrated *through actions*?

d. How important do you think actions are to your faith?

5. Describe "I can't, but He can" faith, which is based on the story of blind Bartimaeus (see Mark 10:46–52).

a. How does this story show "reckless faith"?

b. What should be our response to opposition when we are praying for healing?

ACTIVATION EXERCISE

Based on where your group/class is at, you could consider a variety of different options in moving forward. If the group/class is part of a church, be sure to consult the leadership before engaging any of the following options:

- Go out in teams to pray for the sick in the local community or outreach.

- Go out in teams to hospitals and pray for the sick.

- For further training, you can attend an upcoming Global Awakening School of Healing (visit the website at www.globalawakening.com to see when and where future schools will be held).

WEEKLY READING ASSIGNMENT

Be sure to read Chapter 20 in *Power to Heal* this week and complete your study guide assignments. Instead of interactive assignments/discussion questions, you will receive prayer directives and scripts that will help you pray for people at different levels of faith.

You will review the four expressions of faith in the Gospel of Mark and learn how to pray based on these specific examples. The actual biblical accounts are described in much greater detail in the *Power to Heal* book and video sessions.

SESSION NOTES

JESUS STILL WORKS WITH DIFFERENT LEVELS OF FAITH

These four kinds of faith are not unchangeable, timeless laws. They are not binding. I think you will see that in each of the Gospel accounts we study, God has both confirmed these valid expressions of faith and He has moved beyond them.

Consider these more of a roadmap or blueprint than a fixed formula. I want you to be aware of the different levels of faith people may demonstrate during the healing process, because knowing this gives you the ability to work specifically with different faith levels. When you take people through the five-step prayer model, or have the chance to pray for them on the spot, their level of faith will actually give you a starting place for how to pray. Knowing this gives you the advantage, since their faith indicates what you have to work with.

We will finish our study together by reviewing the four kinds of faith demonstrated in the book of Mark. My prayer is that, through these sessions together, you have been taken on a journey from activation to perseverance to increased revelation. These three steps go together. The five-step prayer model, along with cornerstone truths of testimony and intimacy with God, get you activated. Learning lessons like the agony of defeat and the thrill of victory help you to persevere in a lifestyle of healing ministry. Words of knowledge and four levels of faith bring you into increased revelation. Words of knowledge give you access to information about a condition or sickness you could not know through natural, human means, while identifying the four levels of healing gives you divine insight on how to work with people who need healing prayer.

You will find it interesting that Jesus Himself worked with people at different faith levels. This immediately dispels the myth that "you won't get healed if you don't have enough faith." Don't misunderstand me, faith is very important. I say it time after time—the more faith, the more that happens. The more faith in a person, the more likely he or she will receive healing; the more faith that is being expressed in an atmosphere, the more likely it will be that waves of healing will break out among that specific group of people. Faith is important; I just never want it to become a stumbling block, preventing you from praying for a person in need.

ACTIVATE

Over the next four days, I will be giving you prayer blueprints and directives based on the four kinds of faith demonstrated in the book of Mark. These entries will help you practically apply each story to different situations you come across and show you how to lead different people in healing prayer.

VERY WEAK FAITH: "IF YOU CAN"

READ MARK 9:17–29
(Father and His Demonized Son)

How do we know when a sickness may be demonic? Here are some clues:

- You have pain that moves when you are prayed for.

- You have pain that gets worse when you are prayed for.

- You have pain that the doctors cannot diagnose or determine the cause.

- You have pain that medication should relieve, but it does not.

- You have pain that gets worse when you come to church or that you become more aware of in a service.

In almost all of these circumstances, an afflicting spirit causes the problem.

PRAYER DIRECTIVES

If people think they have a condition that might be caused by an afflicting spirit, or they admit to having only a little faith—like the man with the demonized son—it's time for you to pray for them. Encourage people to be honest about their level of faith. Encourage the person to pray the following prayer out loud. It's simple—just one line. Ask the person to repeat: "Jesus, if You can do anything, take pity on me and heal me."

You Can Use the Following Language to Help Lead People in Healing Prayer:

Now I want to remind you what Jesus said. *"If I can do anything? All things are possible to him who believes."* Now, pray this way: "Lord, I believe. Help my unbelief." My desire for you is that in the name of Jesus Christ, God the Father will answer your prayer; that He will help your unbelief.

And now pray this:

"Lord, in the name of Jesus, I command every spirit of affliction to leave. I break your power now in Jesus's name. I cancel your assignment, and I command you to leave now. Come, Holy Spirit, and increase my faith, increase my awareness of Your presence. Enable me to receive Your blessing and cause Your healing to flow into my body in the name of Jesus."

If you have a witness of the power of God that touched your body when you prayed this prayer, or you can tell you've been healed, or you felt something lift off you, then thank Jesus for what He has done. If your healing has not fully manifested or you have another need, then keep praying.

SOME FAITH: "IF YOU ARE WILLING"

~~~

READ MARK 1:40–42
(the Man with Leprosy)

PRAYER DIRECTIVES

If a person has something wrong with the skin, or a skin disorder of any kind, you should share the Mark 1:40–42 story with them. Or if the prayee's faith level matches this man with leprosy—the person believes that God *can* heal, but he or she just doesn't know if He *wants* to heal—encourage the person that this is the time for healing since God can absolutely work with that level of faith.

Encourage the Person Using These Words:

Here is what I want you to pray. I want you to close your eyes and picture that Jesus Christ is right in front of you, because in faith He is. I want you to pray this prayer out loud:

"Jesus, if You are willing, You can heal me."

Now I want you to remember what Jesus said to the man with leprosy: "I am willing." Let Jesus's words sink into your heart. Hear those words spoken especially for you! "I am willing," Jesus says.

My desire for you is that God will hear your prayer and that the hand of Jesus will come down upon you. In Jesus's name, I pray that you will know and sense the presence of God touching you. I bless you in Jesus's name, and pray that you will move from hope into faith and into the fullness of your healing.

GREAT FAITH: "IF I CAN"

READ MARK 5:34–34

PRAYER DIRECTIVES

If the person you are praying for has something wrong with the blood—AIDS, hepatitis A, B, C, high blood pressure, low blood pressure, anemia, too much fat in the blood, high cholesterol, or any other type of disease carried in the blood—this is a very relevant story. Also, if the person needs healing—and his or her faith level is like the woman with the issue of blood, where the person knows that Jesus can do anything and that He is willing to heal them—you need to look and listen for that level of expectancy.

Encourage the Person with These Words:

If this story represents where you are—in need of a healing for a blood disorder or you are ready to touch the hem of Jesus's robe to receive your healing—then I want you to close your eyes. As you close your eyes, I want you to picture Jesus, the Son of God, walking in front of you. As you picture Him, purpose in your heart: "This is my chance." Then extend your hand, with a believing expectancy, toward Jesus, believing by faith that you are going to touch Him. When you lean forward to touch Him in this act of faith, His virtue is going to flow into you for healing.

My prayer for you is that as you are leaning in to touch Jesus, God the Father will release healing virtue to you. I pray that the anointing that flowed out of Jesus into that woman will flow into you and cause healing to come to your body in the name of Jesus. In the name of Jesus, I bless you, and I speak healing to your body as God's power comes into you.

As you are reaching out to Jesus, I speak healing to your blood, to your liver. I come against any disease in the name of Jesus—AIDS, HIV, hepatitis A, B, and C. I pray that the purifying power of God would go through your liver and your heart, through your whole circulatory system in Jesus's name. In Jesus's name, I command high blood pressure to come down and low blood pressure to come up and iron levels to register normal. I bless your blood in every way that every disease would be healed.

If, as you pictured Jesus and reached out to touch Him, you felt that healing virtue or any other sign of God's power touching you, thank the Lord for what He has done and is doing in your body. Ask Him to continue to touch you and make you whole.

RECKLESS FAITH: "I CAN'T, BUT HE CAN"

READ MARK 10:46–52

Encourage the Person Using These Words:

Bartimaeus's story is your story too, if you have trouble with your eyes—legally blind, near-sighted, far-sighted, or astigmatism. And here's the prayer—I want you to pray the one that blind Bartimaeus prayed. Say out loud, "Jesus, Son of David, have mercy on me." Say it again: "Jesus, Son of David, have mercy on me."

Now here is my prayer for you. In Jesus's name, I bless your eyes. Father, I ask You to hear their cry for mercy. Hear this cry and touch eyes that need healing. Glorify Your name, Lord, by bringing healing.

As you are crying out for Jesus to have mercy on you, I want you to picture Him right in front of you, and He is coming to you and you want to see. Jesus said, "Go. Your faith has healed you." As you receive His touch and your healing, thank the Lord for what He has done and is currently doing in and through you, and share with others the mercy He has had on you.

SOME BASIC CAUTIONS FOR HEALING MINISTRY

LISTEN TO THE VOICE OF THE HOLY SPIRIT AND OBEY HIM

In Matthew 7:21–23, these words of the Lord are recorded:

Not everyone who says to Me, "Lord, Lord," shall enter the kingdom of heaven, but he who does the will of My Father in heaven. Many will say to Me in that day, "Lord, Lord, have we not prophesied in Your name, cast out demons in Your name, and done many wonders in Your name?" And then I will declare to them, "I never knew you; depart from Me, you who practice lawlessness!" (Matthew 7:21–23)

The Lord seems to say that the exercise of great spiritual power, even in His own name, is not necessarily in accordance with the will of God. If not, it is regarded by the Lord as lawlessness. What does it mean to be *lawless* in this context? It is not referring to adhering to the Mosaic Law or Torah. Those who are lawless do not listen to God. They hear but do not obey. They might perform supernatural exploits in the name of Jesus, but their lives do not consistently demonstrate one who is yielded, submitted, and following the Lord. This does not imply perfection, nor does it mean you should wait until you are 100 percent "cleaned up" in order to be used in the healing ministry. It simply means that the posture of your heart should be one that listens to the Spirit and follows His leading to the best of your ability.

Listening to the Holy Spirit and obedience to His leading are essential to this ministry.

DON'T TAKE CREDIT FOR HEALINGS—
IT'S HIS POWER, NOT YOURS

Peter must be our example here. After he and John healed the lame man in the temple, many excited people who witnessed or heard about the miracle crowded around them. This would have been a fantastic opportunity for them to let pride get the best of them and start welcoming the fame that the miracle could have ushered them into.

However, they chose the opposite. In fact, their decision to divert the focus to Jesus not only took eyes off of them, but it ultimately got them into trouble with the religious leaders who, later on, threatened them not to preach in Jesus's name. Peter said,

> *Men of Israel, why do you marvel at this? Or why look so intently at us, as though by our own power or godliness we had made this man walk? ...And [Jesus's] name, through faith in His name, has made this man strong, whom you see and know* (Acts 3:12,16).

Peter later repeated this statement to the high priest, rulers, elders, and scribes who asked him by what authority or by what name he and John had healed the lame man. Again, Peter said,

> *If we this day are judged for a good deed done to the helpless man, by what means he has been made well, let it be known to you all, and to all the people of Israel, that by the name of Jesus Christ of Nazareth, whom you crucified, whom God raised from the dead, by Him this man stands here before you whole* (Acts 4:9–10).

DO NOT BE DISCOURAGED: NOT EVERYONE YOU PRAY FOR WILL GET HEALED

Paul reminds us of this when he wrote to Timothy: *"Trophimus I have left in Miletus sick"* (2 Tim. 4:20). Surely Paul and others had prayed for Trophimus, but he was not healed. Some see this as a stumbling block for healing ministry. Biblically speaking, however, there is no reason it should be. The Word of God clearly instructs us to pray for healing, regardless of what end-results we experience.

Most likely not everyone you pray for will be healed. We should not take credit for the Lord's healing, and, although we may pray for greater anointing for healing, we should not take on guilt when He chooses not to heal through our prayers at any particular time.

LOVE IS MOST IMPORTANT

Most important of all, in First Corinthians 13 Paul makes it clear that love is important beyond all else. He writes,

> *Though I speak with the tongues of men and of angels, but have not love, I have become sounding brass or a clanging cymbal. And though I have the gift of prophecy, and understand all mysteries and all knowledge, and though I have all faith, so that I could remove mountains, but have not love, I am nothing. And though I bestow all*

my goods to feed the poor, and though I give my body to be burned, but have not love,
it profits me nothing (1 Corinthians 13:1–3).

These passages seem to make it clear that the most important element in any ministry, including a ministry of healing, is love. Healing may seem to be a compassionate activity in its essence, but it can be practiced with various motivations. The believer who engages in any ministry should pray for the gift of receiving the love of God, and for becoming a channel of God's love to flow to those we minister to.

PRELIMINARIES FOR PRAYING FOR HEALING

At step three in the five-step prayer model, you are in the process of praying for the prayee's condition. While doing so, it is important for you to be mindful of other situations the prayee is going through that might prevent him or her from receiving healing.

God can do anything. By grace, He is consistently overriding systems and principles, healing those who seemingly do not deserve it or who are not "cleaned up." By and large, however, these are some key hindrances that should be removed so a person can be ideally positioned to receive healing.

FORGIVENESS OF ANOTHER'S WRONG CONDUCT

If it appears that someone else caused the condition, or that someone wronged the person around the time the condition started, find out if the sick person has forgiven the other who has wronged them. If not, forgiveness should precede your prayer for healing. Unforgiveness can be a major obstacle to healing. If you think forgiveness is called for, ask the sick person to forgive the offending individual, even if the sick person is not aware of any resentment toward that person.

REPENTANCE FOR ONE'S OWN WRONG CONDUCT AND ASKING FORGIVENESS FOR IT

If it appears that the condition was brought on by sin, very gently inquire if the person agrees that this might be so. If he does, encourage him to repent and ask God's forgiveness. This should precede your prayer for healing. Sin that is not repented of can impede healing. Anger can contribute to back pain and some forms of depression. Likewise, smoking might have been the cause of lung cancer.

But be tender here. Ask if perhaps the condition could be related to his lifestyle, or perhaps say, "I wonder if this condition could be related to things you have done in the past." Never accuse the person confrontationally of causing his or her condition by their sin. It is seldom helpful, and there is always the chance that you may be wrong.

A caution is needed here: If this leading is of the Holy Spirit, the Holy Spirit will usually indicate the specific sin which is the problem, not sin in general. General accusations of sin are often destructive, and probably are from the enemy. A person may need to forgive himself. He may have caused his own injury or sickness. This may seem unnecessary, but it sometimes releases healing.

AN ATTITUDE OF RECEIVING

Ask the person not to pray while you are praying for him or her. Here again, be gentle and loving. Say something like: "I know this means a lot to you, and you have probably prayed a lot about your condition, but for now I need you to focus on your body. I want you to just relax and to let me know if anything begins to happen in your body, like heat, tingling, electricity, a change in the amount or location of the pain, etc. If you are praying in English or in tongues, or thanking Jesus, or saying "Yes, Yes!" it is harder for you to focus on your body, and it is harder for you to receive healing. Sometimes a person may find it very hard not to pray. Don't be hung up on this. Pray anyway.

NOTES

WATCH GOD ACCOMPLISH
THE MIRACULOUS

THROUGH YOU.

LEARN FROM DR. RANDY CLARK!

Every Christian has been sent and empowered by Jesus to heal the sick. The problem is that many of us don't know how to practically complete this task.

In the *Power to Heal* curriculum, international evangelist, teacher, and apostolic voice, Dr. Randy Clark, shares eight practical, Bible-based tools that will help you start praying for the sick and see them supernaturally healed!

THE HOLY SPIRIT
WANTS TO WORK THROUGH YOU!

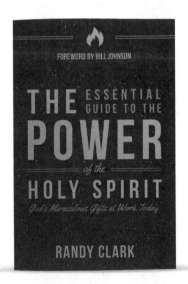

MANY CHRISTIANS HAVE EMBRACED THE DECEPTION THAT THE HOLY SPIRIT IS NO LONGER AT WORK.

But Dr. Randy Clark, President and Founder of Global Awakening, has been an *eyewitness* to the miraculous work of the Holy Spirit and a *key participant* in watching Him powerfully transform lives throughout the world. In this easy-to-read guide, he equips believers to understand and walk in the power of the Spirit every day.

- Discover the gifts of the Holy Spirit that are available to you.

- Recognize an authentic move of God in your church, community, & life.

- Understand how miracles, signs, and wonders play a key role evangelism.

FULFILL YOUR DESTINY! UNLOCK THE POWER OF THE HOLY SPIRIT IN YOUR LIFE.

Christian Prophetic
CERTIFICATION PROGRAM

We are happy to announce the launch of the
**Christian Prophetic Certification Program
(CPCP).**

CPCP will teach students how to recognize the gift of prophecy in
their own life, allowing them to better recognize communications
from the Holy Spirit.

Students will gain a truly Biblical perspective on the prophetic both
from the Old and New Testaments. They will also learn about the
history of prophesy within the church, its benefits and the ways in
which it went off track.

**Courses are available online
and can be taken anywhere at any time.**

Check out our website for more details at
propheticcertification.com

JOIN US!

globalawakening
lighting fires • building bridges • casting vision

Based in Mechanicsburg, PA, the Apostolic Network of Global Awakening (ANGA) is a teaching, healing and impartation ministry with a heart for the nations. Founded in 1994 by Randy Clark after his involvement with the Toronto Airport Christian Fellowship revival, the ministry exists to fulfill the biblical commissions of Jesus:

> *As you go preach, saying the Kingdom of heaven is at hand. Heal the sick, cleanse the lepers, raise the dead, cast out demons. Freely you have received, freely give (Matthew 10:7-8).*

> *Therefore go and make disciples of all nations, baptizing them in the name of the Father and of the Son and of the Holy Spirit, and teaching them to obey everything I have commanded you. And surely I am with you always, to the very end of the age (Matthew 28:19-20).*

Through the formation of ANGA, International Ministry Trips (IMT), the Schools of Healing and Impartation and the Global School of Supernatural Ministry, Global Awakening offers training, conferences, humanitarian aid, and ministry trips in an effort to raise up a company of men and women who will facilitate revival among the nation's leaders. By providing an assortment of international training opportunities, the ministry works in accordance with the revelation to the Apostle Paul regarding the purpose of the five fold ministries:

> *It was He who gave some to be apostles, some to be prophets, some to be evangelists, and some to be pastors and teachers, to prepare God's people for works of service, so that the body of Christ may be built up until we all reach unity in the faith and in the knowledge of the Son of God and become mature, attaining to the whole measure of the fullness of Christ (Ephesians 4:11-13).*

Led by Rev. Randy Clark, the ministry has visited over 36 countries and continues to travel extensively to bring hope, healing, and power to the nations.

globalawakening.com